Digital Brand Romance

Digital Brand Romance

*How to Create Lasting Relationships
in a Digital World*

Anna Harrison

BEP

BUSINESS EXPERT PRESS

Leader in applied, concise business books

Description

Tomorrow arrived, and all great relationships now begin online—including the ones between your future customer and your brand. Whether you are selling shoes, software, or spaceship parts, the romance begins and evolves in a digital world. While over 80 percent of businesses think they provide excellent customer experiences only 8 percent of customers agree. The reality is that the state of modern, digital brand relationships is quite dysfunctional: an average conversion rate of 3 percent means that 97 percent of engagements with your brand fail. Not only does this inefficiency chew up marketing budget but it also taints future engagements with your brand.

In *Digital Brand Romance*, you will learn the proprietary six-step ADORE process™ that has helped brands worldwide consistently achieve conversion rates above 20 percent. The ADORE process™ is used by some of the most innovative scaleups, fast-growth exporters, and leading brands to consistently sell more, more often. Each step of the ADORE process™ aligns with one of the key moments of influence in the digital relationship with your brand. Understanding the forces that drive each moment will allow you to identify signs of relationship breakdown; common causes of issues and how to resolve them; and which metrics to track to measure progress. You will also learn how to apply the process to conduct regular digital relationship audits, removing your reliance on luck in the future success of your brand.

Digital Brand Romance is highly practical and offers tactical, helpful advice to apply in your business immediately.

Keywords

digital marketing; product design; growth; scale; CX; customer experience; SEO; search engine optimization; CRO; conversion rate optimization; digital audit; journey orchestration; ADORE process™

Contents

Testimonials

Foreword

In 1999 I got my first real education into online commerce when the marketing lead and the technology lead of the company I was running let me know, as a side-hustle, they'd been experimenting with selling wine online. At the time, I thought it sounded like an interesting idea that would make them earn a little extra cash and would help us all to learn more about the mysteries of online commerce. The business grew rapidly, became a significant player in the industry, generated millions of dollars for its owners, and is still operating successfully 22 years later.

Why is that story relevant to *Digital Brand Romance*? Because in 1999 I can remember the most significant learning from my colleagues' wine business was that the key to success was not the technology, and it wasn't the wine quality—the key to success was their consumer base and the extent to which they understood and exceeded their needs.

Reading *Digital Brand Romance* brought that learning back to me as I reflected on how many of us, including me, make the mistake of seeing digital commerce as something so dynamic and magical that we simply can't keep up. In this book, Anna Harrison brings us back to the reality that through looking at the data available, applying a systematic process, and making simple improvements to our digital approach we can remove the mystery and deliver an experience that exceeds our customer expectations and helps our companies succeed.

Unsurprisingly, given the COVID pandemic, we've been living through I first met Anna via Zoom while I was in lockdown in Auckland. Anna had recently started working as one of New Zealand Trade and Enterprise's (NZTE) private-sector advisors and was specifically working with our customer companies to help them improve their digital commerce capability. Even over Zoom, it was easy to be infected by Anna's enthusiasm for the work she was doing and not long after that call I started hearing how much our customers were appreciating Anna's enthusiasm and her advice. Soon after that I was hearing of game-changing turnarounds in our customers' results. What was going on?

It turns out that Anna had a bunch of ideas and frameworks she was working through with our customers. These were a distillation of Anna's extensive research of time-honored literature on topics like buyer behavior, contemporary reading on the impact of technology, and then combined with real-life experiments and execution with companies of all sizes and in many sectors. In this book, Anna brings this knowledge and experience together to present a way for any company to improve their digital connection to their customers.

The vast majority of companies we work with at NZTE are tiny on the world stage. They don't have teams of marketing people and only a few of them would have dedicated digital marketing expertise so they need advice and processes they can implement quickly. In the development of the ADORE process™ outlined in this book, Anna delivers exactly that: a practical, systematic, guide for analyzing performance and then addressing each part of your digital commerce approach.

I'm thrilled that Anna continues to support our customers and I'm thrilled that many more companies can now access the ADORE process™ and tools through reading and applying the learning Anna shares in *Digital Brand Romance.*

—Glen Murphy
Regional Director, Australia Pacific
New Zealand Trade and Enterprise
August 2021

Why This. Why You. Why Now

Simon says we should start with why (Sinek 2009). Attention is one of the scarcest resources on the planet, the driver behind modern economics, and a global leveler. Each day, regardless of where you wake up, you awaken to a fixed set of hours at your disposal. The primary objective of every other entity on this planet is to consume a portion of your available attention. This is entirely my goal too: I have at most one more paragraph to quietly convince you that this is the one book you should read this year, that reading this book will give you an edge over your competition, and that you can't afford to delay. Tick tock.

Brutal transparency, unique vision, and clarity of thought are often cited as my superpowers. An odd combination to hang your cape on, but these are the tools with which I have toiled for 10,000+ hours, mastering my craft. I have worked with clients around the world, from leading brands to startups in almost every industry. I have listened to their stories, deconstructed their successes and failings, and reconstructed them as repeatable and scalable pathways for growth. With their help, I have created a proven formula for success in a digital space—a consistent way to sell more, more often. My *why* is because this is where my passion and expertise lie. Your *why* is because you can't afford not to know.

Digital Is the New Normal

It is 2021. Millennials are almost 40 years old, and the world is hungover from the COVID-19 pandemic. A decade of behavioral change took place while we were socially distancing. I ran into your grandmother at the park yesterday. She showed me how e-commerce works. Digital is so much the new normal that in only a year, the phrase has already become banal.

Moore's law (Moore 1965) has conditioned us to be amazed at the pace of technological change. Each decade, tomorrow's technology is served up yesterday. Blink, and supercomputers are replaced by cell phones. Blink,

Early market   Mainstream market

The chasm

Tech enthusiasts (14%)   Early majority (34%)

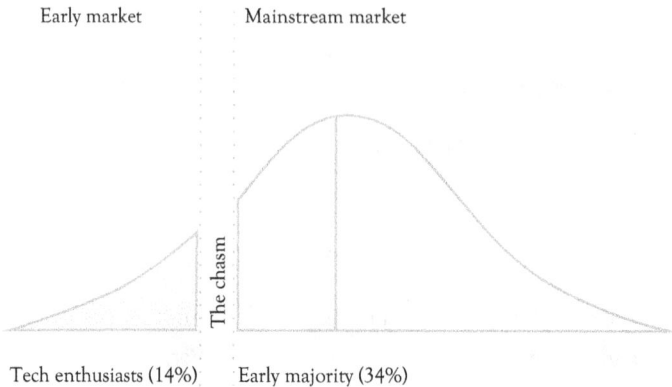

Figure 0.1 Rogers technology adoption curve

and cell phones are replaced—perhaps we can't imagine what will replace them, but we fully expect that we will be amazed.

In contrast, the rate of change in human behavior is staggeringly slow. Researchers dedicate careers to unraveling the science behind this and still can't tell us why it's easier to eat a doughnut than get up at 4:44 a.m. on a Monday to run 10 km in the cold. Rogers technology adoption curve (Figure 0.1) quantifies our propensity for inertia: only 14 percent of the population is willing to try something new (Bohlen and Beal 1957). Everyone else wants to be a follower, ideally, a third or fourth follower. Even the first follower position is remarkably unpopular.

And then a shift. A tsunami out of nowhere resets our expectations. Fear of getting sick and the pragmatics of being housebound leave us with no option but to adapt. And we do. According to McKinsey's "The Great Acceleration" (2020), more goods were traded online in the first 90 days of the pandemic than in the preceding decade. Google predicts that around 60 percent of all global spending will be digital by 2024. Mired executives find themselves repeating a new refrain to colleagues over Zoom calls "What I thought was impossible, we achieved in two weeks."

The Shift Is Permanent

Although COVID-19 was a catalyst for the step change in human behavior, the effects of these changes are here to stay (Taniguchi 2021).

In parts of the world that have returned to "normal," indications are that the shift to digital is permanent (Manu 2017). The Reserve Bank of Australia has reported that 30 percent of Australian households now prefer to engage and shop online, despite having the freedom to choose to shop in person (Australia, being both an island and at the very end of the universe, is fortunate to have had a very mild case of the pandemic by global standards).

> *I think we all now understand that anyone will buy anything online, given the right experience, and if your retail model is based on being an endpoint to a logistics chain then you have an existential problem.*
> —Benedict Evans, Resetting Online Commerce

The writing on the wall is unmistakable. The large "millennial" consumer group, and those younger, are characterized as having high expectations and brutal disloyalty (Ordun 2015). Global conditions have accelerated the technology adoption curve, bringing the laggards online. Google research reports that over 84 percent of all purchases *prior to the pandemic*, including consumer and enterprise purchases, originated online. They even have a name for the moment of first contact—the zero moment of truth (ZMOT) (Lecinski 2011). Without exception, the first point of contact between your brand and your future customer will happen in a digital space (Figure 0.2).

Imagine this. You are a junior engineer in your first week of a new job. Your boss tasks you with researching options for industrial radial sprayers to specify on a large client job. You Google "industrial radial sprayers" and begin your search. What happens next? Remember that I don't know you, but I do know with reasonable certainty that this is what you will do: you will look at the search results displayed on the first page and open a few links into new tabs. You will navigate to each new tab, giving it a quick once-over and decide in a matter of seconds whether you will continue to research that brand or go back to Google and search for something new.

Chief executive Mark Coulter said recent trading suggested COVID-19 had permanently accelerated the adoption of online shopping in the furniture and homewares market.

Early market   Mainstream market

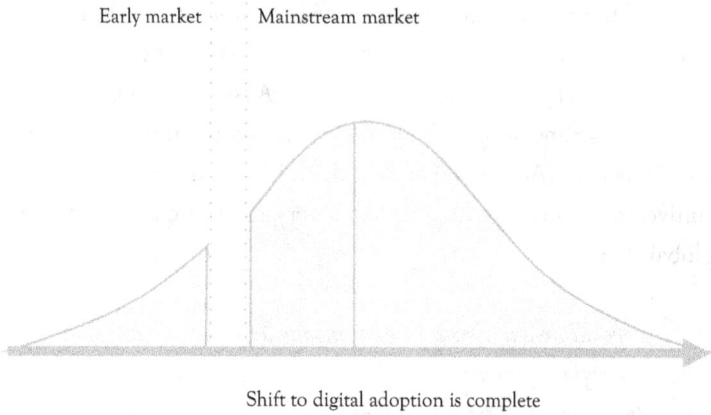

Shift to digital adoption is complete

Figure 0.2 The shift to digital is complete: The mainstream market has adopted digital as the starting point for buying journeys

You only need to look at the US to see how the e-commerce market is playing out, and why we remain bullish about the shift from offline to online. We are at the start of this once-in-a-generation shift (to online shopping).

—Mark Coulter, CEO, Temple & Webster

Over 90 percent of all traffic on the Internet originates on page one of Google. A corollary to that statistic is that content not listed on page one of Google gets close to no traffic. The odds of the junior engineer investigating your brand are overwhelmingly not in your favor.

On the one hand, we know that the relationship between your brand and a new customer will begin in a digital space. On the other, the odds that the new customer will find you and then give you more than a cursory glance are reasonably close to zero.

In *Modern Romance* (Ansari and Klinenberg 2016), comedian Aziz Ansari reports on research conducted by Columbia University into the "new world" of dating. Long story short—at any moment, should you choose to, you can access over two billion potential dates right in your phone, and yet, conversion rates from these apps are regularly very low, circa 3 percent for the top performers. In a commercial context, we have been conditioned to expect that 3 percent conversion rates are "good,"

Google
$147B

Facebook
$30B

2010   2020

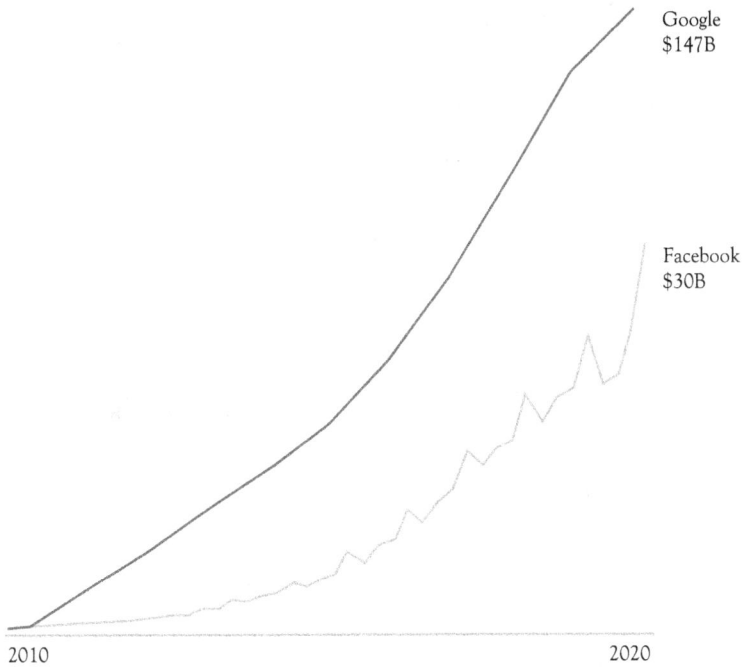

Figure 0.3 Global ad revenue for Facebook and Google

an assumption that delivers hockey-stick growth to those selling ads, not those buying ads (Figure 0.3).

In real life, you need to be strategic about finding a relationship in your phone, converting it and then making it last. To a large extent, we understand how to optimize each of these three stages in real life. In business, the industry is vigilantly focused on finding new potential relationships (Ross and Tyler 2011) and pays relatively little attention to what happens next.

> *The consumer experience is rapidly evolving from one that's built upon the transactional process of in-store shopping to one that's rooted in deep, ongoing and enriching relationships.*
> —Harvard Business Review 2021

The part of the process where the value lies—the conversion and long-term maintenance of the relationship—has not yet been optimized at scale. Although we know that loyalty delivers 2.5 times more revenue (Markey 2020), we simply have not yet devised a formula for consistently and systematically creating digital spaces that encourage and enhance the formation and evolution of relationships between brands and site visitors.

Expectations Unmet

While human behavior has shifted, business change has not followed suit at the same pace. Consumer expectations currently exceed what brands are delivering. Case in point: Forbes reports that 80 percent of businesses think they deliver exceptional customer experiences—yet only 8 percent of their customers agree. These conditions are ideal for large-scale customer dissatisfaction.

Customer satisfaction is subjective (Harrison 2015). It is a condition or property experienced by a human, and although subjective, it is quantifiable. Satisfaction is the difference between what we expect and what we experience (Figure 0.4)—high expectations and poor experiences lead to dissatisfaction, while moderate expectations and good experiences result in satisfaction.

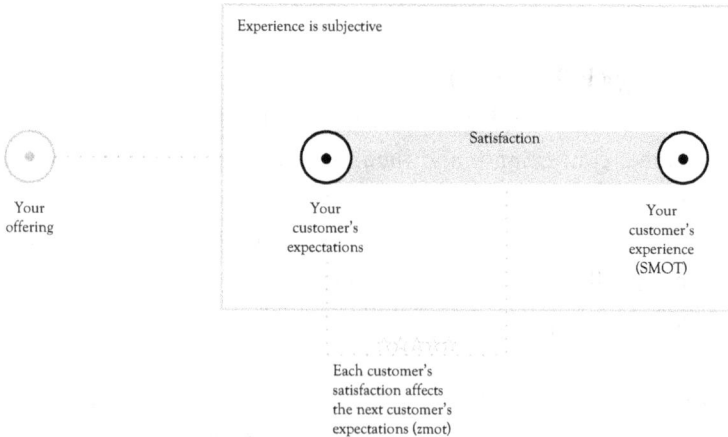

Experience is subjective

Satisfaction

Your
offering

Your
customer's
expectations

Your
customer's
experience
(SMOT)

Each customer's
satisfaction affects
the next customer's
expectations (zmot)

Figure 0.4 Satisfaction is the difference between what we expect and what we experience

Although satisfaction is experienced at a human level, it is a critical factor regardless of whether your brand sells to consumers (B2C), other businesses (B2B), or intermediaries. Ultimately, every commercial transaction is acted out by human beings. A human makes the decision to buy or not to buy. Another human writes reviews about your brand, and recommendations about your business are exchanged between humans. On a larger scale, the way we interact with the world, what we desire, and what we buy is shaped by the policies implemented by companies like Apple and Facebook. From Cambridge Analytica to the "war on data tracking," the choices you make are an outcome of decisions made by the CEOs of these companies. And the policies and choices made by CEOs boil down to their human personalities and mutual relationships.

The level of satisfaction experienced by any one human will impact the future satisfaction of strangers. In real terms, Varga and Alburquerque (*Harvard Business Review* 2020) found that one bad review is all that it took for most new buyers to leave because of introduced uncertainty, and for these departed buyers to spend 16 percent more with a competitor brand. Your next dissatisfied customer is helping your competitor grow.

Your next dissatisfied customer is helping your competitor grow.

Dissatisfaction directly affects revenue by inhibiting your ability to sell more, more often. Your ability to meet customer expectations and consistently create the conditions that will lead to customer satisfaction in a digital space is paramount to business success in the current economy. The brands that get digital romance right succeed. Everyone else either stagnates, folds, or is subsumed by strategic mergers. The size of the prize is enormous too, as reflected by the widening gap in profits between digital leaders and digital laggards (Figure 0.5).

You need to meet or exceed expectations to survive. If you want to sell more shoes, services, cheese, bio-dynamic fertilizers, balloons, peanuts, enterprise marketing solutions, or cases of wine, you need to create conditions in the digital world that will encourage a perfect stranger, the site visitor who lands on your website, to commit to a relationship with your brand. As we have already seen, the odds that this will happen magically are not stacked in your favor.

This book will show you how to do this consistently and systematically, regardless of what industry or sector your business is in.

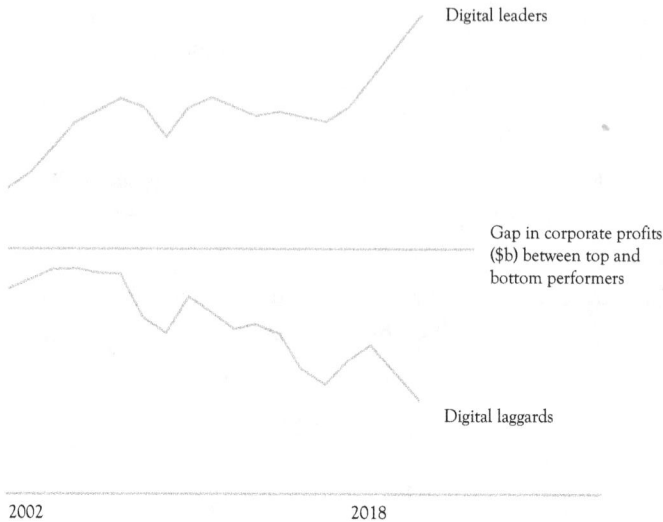

Figure 0.5 Gap in corporate profits between the top and bottom performers

Source: McKinsey, "The Great Acceleration," 2020.

Summary: Short on Time, Read This

I respect that your time is short. While I wake up at 3 a.m. and think about this stuff, you are more likely thinking about how to boost sales in your business, how to unlock new revenue opportunities in your organization, how to get a promotion, or increase returns on your marketing spend. You may be thinking about how to design and optimize the digital footprint of your clients' brands.

If you don't have time to read this book cover to cover, or if you are picking this up again for a quick refresher, here are the highlights:

- Part II describes the ADORE process™ for creating lasting relationships in a digital space. It breaks the relationship between buyer and brand into seven key milestones and shows you how to optimize your brand's digital footprint for each. Each chapter in Part II outlines how to spot issues, understand fundamental causes, and apply proven solutions. If you are short on time, follow the links to the online version of these chapters and use the audit tool to diagnose and improve your digital footprint.

- Part III shows you how to scale the ADORE process™ to increase the performance of your product team. It also shows you how to apply the same process to setting up conditions for successful engagements with external agencies you will likely engage to execute on the work.

- All of the worksheets and diagrams in this book are available to download and use with attribution. The slide pack will save you time if you need to create presentations to your board, explain the framework to your clients or align your product, and marketing teams around the ADORE process™.

PART I

Webonomics, or the Forces That Determine How We Buy

In 1996, Schwartz, a technology writer and former editor of *Business-Week*, coined the term Webonomics: "the study of the production, distribution, and consumption of goods, services, and ideas over the World Wide Web" (Schwartz 1997). Back then, the Internet was "astonishingly inhabited by tens of millions" of users around the world, and we used charming phrases like "World Wide Web" when talking about the new revolution slowly emerging around us. From his prescient vantage point at the beginning of the Internet, Schwartz foretold nine principles that would be critical to business success in the new economic arena. Of the tenets he defined, his recognition that the resource of scarcity in the new economy would be the "ability to command and sustain that attention" was the most prophetic. That he never imagined more than tens of millions of users ever engaging in this economy makes his observation that much more visionary.

Fast forward to today: 4.66 billion active daily users; 100 percent penetration in the under 29-year-old category; even your grandmother has 4.6 social media accounts. The "attention economy" has its own Wikipedia page, and tens of millions of people have watched TED talks on this topic alone. The battle that is being fought every minute of every day in this digital arena is the desire to be seen and loved by the millions of eyeballs walking past each website on Internet Street (Lecinski 2011). And the consumers are winning the fight.

Consumers are in the driver's seat, deciding at scale what the destiny of each brand will be. They are in the process of turning business to consumer (B2C) commerce into consumer to business (C2B). We simply have not noticed the full extent of it yet. Consumers have access to all the information inside their phones. They have adapted and become more sophisticated, easily thwarting sellers' efforts with tabs closed and forgotten at impressive speeds. In the United States, the average citizen is exposed to upwards of 4,000 brands each day. Think about that—4,000 sellers vying for you to choose them from the moment you open your eyes.

Consumers have become experts at ignoring long-standing methods of being sold to. In 2020, 47 percent of consumers were using adblockers, costing U.S. businesses $12.12 billion in lost revenue. In 2021, Apple announced that they would turn off tracking cookies, small data files used to identify site visitors, at the operating system level. The significance of this decision is enormous, as cookies are one of the primary techniques that companies such as Facebook use to follow individuals' online habits when they click around on the Web. Cookies are the reason you keep seeing ads for black turtlenecks, interior design tips and new jobs on every website you visit.

The data stored in the cookies helps advertisers target specific audiences, an activity they pay a premium for. Turning off cookies by default or giving users greater agency over whether they accept cookies or not, has the potential to wipe out significant advertising revenue for companies like Facebook—and significantly change the strategies that sellers can rely on to become seen.

> *Conning the customer won't work. The whole language of branding dissolves in the new media. The logic behind brand differentiation disappears. The new generation of consumers are more sophisticated. Consumers see right through what advertisers are manipulating them into doing. Most people in advertising don't understand that. Advertisers have been getting away with murder.*
>
> —Evan Schwartz, *Webonomics* (1997)

To succeed in business today, it is not enough to provide an outstanding experience. It is not enough to have a cracking marketing team that shepherds significant quantities of site visitors to your website on the promise of 2.35 percent conversion rates. It is not enough to provide efficient transactional encounters, even if you do know the customer's name and basic demographics. To succeed today and well into tomorrow, you need to create conditions that will foster lasting relationships with your customers in a digital space. This book will show you exactly how to do that in Part II. In this section, we look at the building blocks of lasting buyer brand relationships—the timeless forces that influence how we buy, how we make decisions, and how we form relationships.

The Future Is Not Random

It's easy to get confused when thinking about the future. It is a time that has not happened yet, and so, we mistakenly believe, is unpredictable. We forget that the future is a consequence of what is here today, and what is here today is known to us already. In *The Imagination Challenge*, Alexander Manu posits that we can make a reasonable prediction about tomorrow by examining the knowns of today (Manu 2007). The strategy described in the book, used by Manu to de-risk the future state for Fortune 500 companies like Disney, LEGO, and Motorola, is based on the idea of looking at "signals." Some of these signals are fast-moving, such as emerging technologies, while other signals are slow-moving, such as human behaviors. If we understand the mechanics of the slow-moving signals, the ones that impact how we make buying decisions and form relationships, we can not only optimize the digital brand space for today but have confidence that foundational parts will continue to be relevant and effective into the future.

Brand Monogamy, Temporary Fling, or Polyamorous Free for All

Every generation has its own characteristics, shaped by its exposure to world events, trends, technologies, and even diseases. The way we experience life affects our core values, and with that, shapes our attitudes toward how we buy, what elements of the purchase we prioritize, and what or whom we are loyal to (Ordun 2015). Our grandparents were likely loyal to a brand for life: once you chose Tide, you stayed with Tide. You probably have a different set of criteria for choosing washing powder, and ultimately, all the brands you choose to spend your dollars with.

Brand loyalty is the degree to which we exhibit a bias toward choosing a specific brand over alternate brands over time (Jacoby and Kyner 1973). Brand loyalty is, in essence, a commitment between yourself and a brand and is characterized by three components:

1. Satisfaction
2. Relationship
3. Time

It makes perfect sense that we exchange our loyalty, in essence giving up our future freedom to evaluate options when making a choice, only if we have a positive relationship with a brand over time. For example, you may discover a particularly stylish and flattering brand of black turtleneck that you purchase. The said black turtleneck performs well, and you are satisfied with the look, feel, price and style. You wear the turtleneck and get a few compliments from your friends. Next time you need to buy a garment to wear in public, you look around at other options and maybe even buy a black turtleneck from another brand. When the new turtleneck arrives, you will compare it against the original brand you were happy with. The next time you need to buy a black turtleneck, you save yourself some time and order 10 from the first brand that you loved. In the future, whenever a turtleneck needs to be replaced, you return to the brand you are now loyal to. Your effectiveness as a seller of turtlenecks depends entirely on whether you understand what keeps your loyal fans committed to you.

Of the three components of brand loyalty, satisfaction is the only factor you can directly affect as a seller. The relationship that is formed over time with your brand is not within your control. It is the subjective experience that evolves and is experienced by your buyer over the course of engaging with you. Each engagement, however, is evaluated by the buyer through a measure of satisfaction. Although satisfaction is also subjective, it is a function of the expectations held going into the interaction—and expectations can be managed (Figure 1.1).

The quality of an experience is measured as the difference between our perceptions and our expectations of an experience (Harrison 2015). This is the critical part—as a seller, you have zero control over the perceived

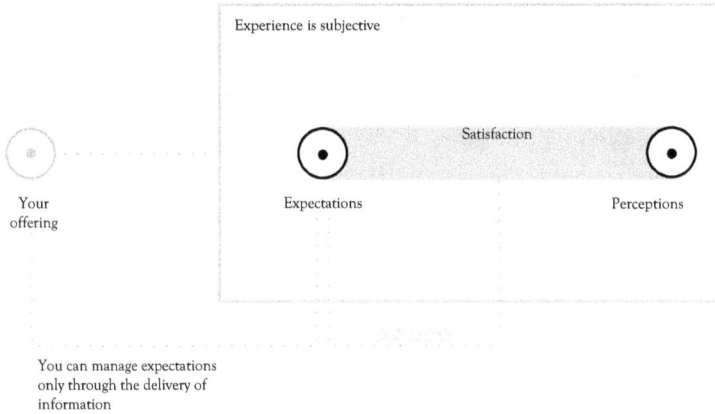

Experience is subjective

Satisfaction

Your offering

Expectations

Perceptions

You can manage expectations
only through the delivery of
information

**Figure 1.1 Satisfaction can be affected through the delivery of
information, which moderates expectations**

experience of a buyer. However, you have a substantial amount of influence over their expected experience. As long as you deliver on what you promised, the promise itself is not important in absolute terms. For example, if I purchase a new black turtleneck online and select the *free* shipping option, I will be delighted if the turtleneck arrives on or before the promised seven days; and I will be very disappointed if it arrives on day 10. As long as the package arrives within the promised time frame, I will be satisfied with the experience. Now, let's say you notice that all your packages are taking eight days to arrive, and your customer complaints are increasing. If you change nothing else other than the copy on your website, from seven to 10 days, you will positively affect the satisfaction of your customers.

Information, when provided at the right time, can be used to control your buyers' expectations, which in turn affects their levels of satisfaction. You have complete agency over the information that you directly provide to your buyers. Your buyers, however, also source information from the collective experience of all your past customers.

Gen Y, or millennials, are the second biggest population in the history of the world (Ordun 2015). This cohort of humanity has already begun to dominate the market, not only because of their own buying power but also because of their influence on their parents and their grip on the purses of their offspring. They are a generation who are natively comfortable with processing large volumes of data, so the "overhead" of reading customer reviews or evaluating multiple alternate brands when making a purchase does not overwhelm them. According to the Google Research team, millennials research everything they buy, down to paperclips and band-aids (Lecinski 2011). Their loyalty is earned when they feel that they have been seen, understood, or connected with—loyalty for them takes the shape of an authentic relationship built on trust. They are perfectly comfortable having this type of relationship with a brand rather than a person.

To influence a millennial buyer once, you need to earn their trust. To induce a millennial buyer to become a lifetime loyal fan, you need to form a trusted relationship with them. The relationship needs to be based on elements they genuinely care about—these buyers are not fools and abhor being "sold" to. Today's consumers desperately want to be seen, known, and respected, and only those brands that "invest in relationships through empathy, deep understanding and insight will prevail" (Ordun 2015).

In a study of factors that affect brand loyalty in millennials (Parment 2013), the researchers found that while these buyers research everything, their decision-making criteria are based on emotion rather than reason. Unlike their parents, when millennials make buying decisions, it is not strictly for reasons that make textbook economic sense. Millennials evaluate risk in terms of social status, not financial loss.

Millennials evaluate risk in terms of social status, not financial loss.

This is a big change in how buying decisions are made today—buyers do not evaluate the features of a product and complete a rational cost/benefits analysis. They often buy in order to feel seen and raise their social standing. They may buy a product entirely because their social media friends recommended it, not because they needed what they purchased. When their expectations are met and they have positive satisfaction, they are proactive in telling their friends about it. Investing in creating strong relationships with your buyers not only affects the primary buyer to brand relationship but, through the collective experiences shared, the satisfaction of future buyers as well.

Why We Buy

Millennials are more aware of their purchasing power and are likely to spend their cash as quickly as they acquire it (der Hovanesian 1999). Given the prevalence of this demographic on the planet and the inherent connectivity and availability of information, we all can access from our cell phones, one could argue that the parts of the world untouched by consumerism are gradually disappearing. Even at the most remote edges of the planet, we can find evidence of the existence and desire to acquire "things"—things like washing machines, fridges, and McDonald's hamburgers. The arc of progress is marked by the acquisition of more. More clothes, more cars, more digital gadgets, and more space to store the spoils of our progress. The process of buying is a familiar activity.

The reasons why we buy are often dressed in layers of complexity and nuance: we are told that we buy to fill a void, we buy because we need, we buy because we want, we buy because we are bored, we buy because we want to belong. We buy to save time, we buy to save money, and we buy to be better in some way (Figure 1.2).

Figure 1.2 Brands want us to think that we buy for a wide range of reasons

Asking the question "why do people buy" in a Google search produces pages of articles entitled "The top X reasons people buy." Wade through the research, the marketing slogans, and the shades of psychology, and at the very core, there is only one reason anyone buys anything: we buy things because they make our lives better.

The only reason anyone buys anything is to make their life better.

If you are in the business of selling, your challenge to sell more, more often reduces to two things:

1. Show your potential buyer how you make their life better, and

2. Deliver on your promise

If you genuinely make their life better and deliver to their expectations, you will have the first step in creating the building blocks of a successful relationship. The mechanics of brand loyalty will take care of the rest, triggering the conditions that will systematically and consistently deliver lasting relationships between your new customers and your brand.

The Mechanics of Brand Loyalty

To understand the mechanics of brand loyalty, we need to understand the basics of how we experience the world and how we determine what makes a particular experience satisfactory. Human experience has been the focus of research for decades. It has been examined from every angle: the self, the collective, the conscious, the subconscious. Our experiences literally define our lives. In line with the arc of progress and consumerism, even the human experience has to some extent been commoditized (Figure 1.3). In 1998, Pine and Gilmore defined "the experience economy" as an emerging era characterized by a new economic offering: experiences. Experiences, like coffee and soya beans, can be bought and sold (Pine and Gilmore 1998).

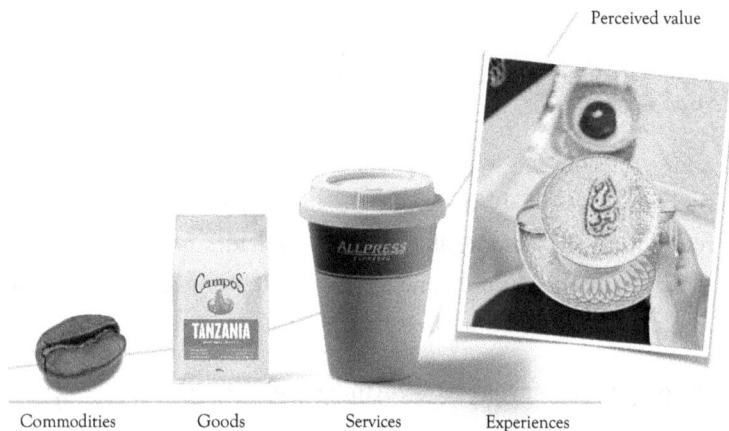

Figure 1.3 Progression of perceived value as commodities are turned into goods, services, and experiences

Experiences, because of their innate value that outlasts the consumption of the cup of coffee, have a much higher intrinsic value. Unlike commodities or simple products and services, experiences continue to deliver value because they take up space in our memories. A simple example—the literal cost of a cup of take-away coffee in a country like Australia is at most $1. This includes the cost of the beans, the cost of the milk, the paper cup, the salary of the Barista, and the fixed costs of the coffee shop. Let's say we purchase a cup of coffee from the same Barista every day for $4.50. The act of buying the coffee, of engaging in familiar banter, of having our order and name remembered transforms the utilitarian cup of coffee into a service, for which we are willing to pay a $3.50 premium. Now think about your everyday coffee—are you compelled to rave about it to your friends? Does that cup of coffee make your list of highlights for the day?

Now close your eyes (only keep them open so you can still read this). Recall the best cup of coffee that you have ever had in your life. Where were you? Who were you with? Was it cold or warm? What were you wearing? What did you smell? That best cup of coffee, which also may have cost $4.50, has actually overdelivered in value as it has become a memory. That best cup of coffee has been etched into your past experience (Figure 1.4).

Research on human memory (Mori 2008; Norman 2009) has shown that past experience, or the memory of an experience, can sometimes be more valuable than the experience itself. Not only does the

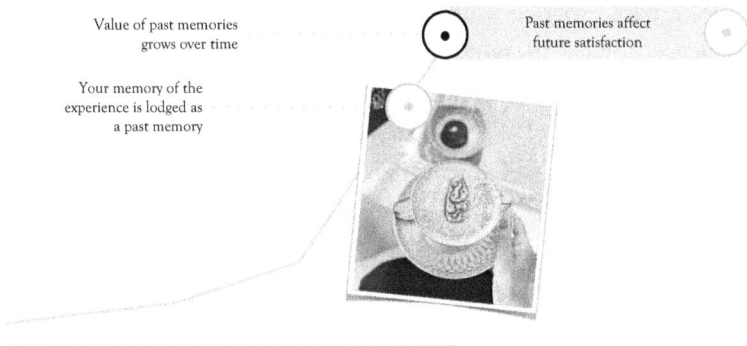

Figure 1.4 The value of past experiences grows over time, positively affecting the future expected experience of others

passing of time serve to delete the bad parts and amplify the good parts of an experience, time can create fake memories, which are indistinguishable from actual memories. In 2009, Don Norman and his colleagues conducted a curious experiment in which they asked visitors to Disney's theme parks about their experience of Bugs Bunny. Participants provided glowing and rave reviews of the wily rabbit, despite the impossibility of the memory (Bugs Bunny is a Warner Bros character, not a Disney one). Even when presented with the evidence, the park goers' enjoyment of the experience was not diminished. The study concluded that the memory of an event was more important than the actual experience (Figure 1.5).

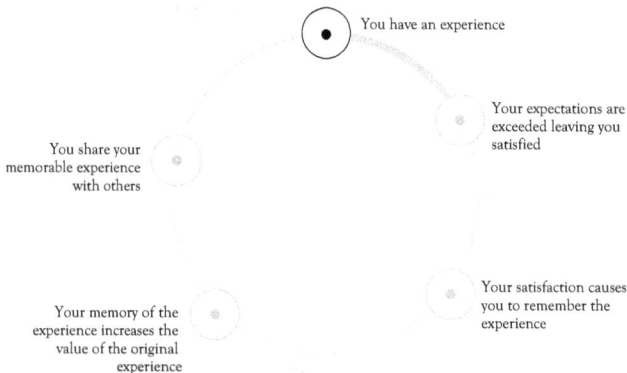

You have an experience

Your expectations are exceeded leaving you satisfied

You share your memorable experience with others

Your satisfaction causes you to remember the experience

Your memory of the experience increases the value of the original experience

Figure 1.5 How your experiences affect your future satisfaction and the experiences of others

Your past experience affects your own perceptions of value or satisfaction and has the power to influence the buying choices of others. In aggregate, your past experience can affect the satisfaction of all future buyers. This is one of the ways in which consumers can, as a cohort, determine the destiny of your brand: the opinion of others is the most influential and powerful impetus to buy (Edelman 2010). Google's ZMOT is the moment where the aggregate public opinion of others influences a new customer's decision to buy. It is the moment where your past experience with a brand has become the inception of the next person's relationship with the brand, setting the mechanics of brand loyalty into motion for another consumer.

Perpetual Brand Loyalty

Fitness is an area of life I have had to work hard at. If we work on the assumption that we all get something in life "for free," the domain of sport and fitness was not the card I was given. Nevertheless, one year I signed up to run a marathon. The preparation that goes into running a marathon is not necessarily exciting. It is a matter of setting a goal and simply chipping away at that goal every single day. The amazing thing is that if you do this, you are guaranteed success. The training involved in running a marathon works, and works for anyone, because the process creates what Jim Collins describes as "the flywheel effect" (Collins 2001).

The flywheel effect is a way to describe the mechanics of a process that works, and because it works, it sets the process into motion again, perpetually (Figure 1.6). A simple fitness flywheel might look like this: I go out and exercise each morning. This makes me feel energized and good about myself. Feeling energized and positive sets my mind up to come up with creative ideas. My creative ideas generate cash flow. Cashflow gives me time to exercise, and the cycle repeats.

There is no single step in the flywheel that is most important or is the one that constitutes the big win or the big breakthrough. The flywheel works because the completion of each step "can't help but" set the next step in motion. There are, unfortunately, no shortcuts in the flywheel: skipping a step breaks the flow of perpetual motion. The flywheel works

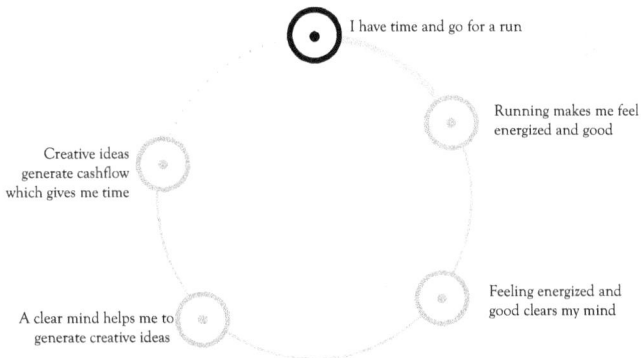

I have time and go for a run

Running makes me feel energized and good

Creative ideas generate cashflow which gives me time

Feeling energized and good clears my mind

A clear mind helps me to generate creative ideas

Figure 1.6 My flywheel is kept in motion when I use time to exercise, clear my mind, generate ideas, and convert these into cashflow

only if you consistently and systematically do the work in each step. If you have never run, there is no single training session that you can do to be marathon ready. You have to do the work each day, and in return, the flywheel will guarantee your success.

The mechanics of brand loyalty work because they create a flywheel of perpetual motion. If you create a beautiful and engaging digital presence, and you address and alleviate anxieties, and you articulate how you make life better for your site visitors, then there is a good chance that the buyers will connect with your brand. The connection will lead to them deciding to purchase from you. The purchase experience will leave the buyer satisfied, and their satisfaction will entice them to share their experience with others. When others learn about your brand, they will visit your website, and the process will start again (Figure 1.7).

A break in the flywheel, or an unfavorable experience at any of the steps, will not only break the perpetual motion of the flywheel, but it can also lead to a new, negative flywheel being started. We see this all the time in fitness, where a break in routine training can lead to the start of a negative cycle of deteriorating fitness. Evidence abounds in commercial contexts too, where a negative experience causes a loyal customer to switch brands. The current state of the banking industry is a great example, where poor customer experiences offered by banks is seeing lifetime customers defect to emerging fintechs and neobanks.

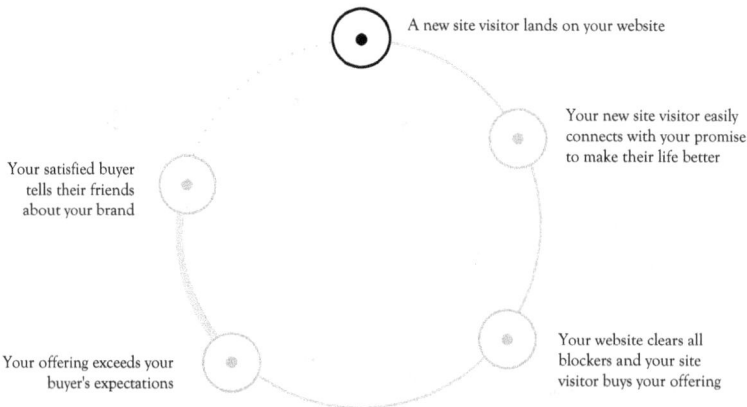

A new site visitor lands on your website

Your new site visitor easily connects with your promise to make their life better

Your website clears all blockers and your site visitor buys your offering

Your offering exceeds your buyer's expectations

Your satisfied buyer tells their friends about your brand

Figure 1.7 The mechanics of brand loyalty: your website draws your new site visitor into a relationship with your brand, your offering exceeds expectations, which compels your buyer to tell their friends, which in turn drives new buyers to your website

The cost of negative experiences and breaks in the flywheel affect not only the buyer but also the opinions of future buyers. In real terms, one negative review is all that it takes for 51 percent of potential buyers to abandon the brand because of the uncertainty introduced and for those defected buyers to spend up to 16 percent more with competitors (*Harvard Business Review* 2020). Think about that—when you leave open the opportunity for a negative review, you are effectively helping your competitors outcompete you. In a larger sense, the Harvard research shows that brands with loyal customers grow revenue 2.5 times faster than brands with one-off, transactional buyers (Markey 2020). Quelch and Jocz show that brands with repeat customers and loyal fans are far more recession-proof and able to sustain more challenging economic times and downturns than competitors (Quelch and Jocz 2009). Billionaire John Paul DeJoria, founder of Paul Mitchell, sums it up nicely: "If you want to sell something, don't be in the selling business. Be in the reorder business."

Recall from the discussion on satisfaction that information moderates the expectations, and in turn, the satisfaction, that buyers have of an experience with your brand. Important to note that this does not mean that every experience with your brand needs to be positive—buyers will tolerate mistakes, delays, and all kinds of things going wrong as long as they are given the right information at the right time (Norman 2009).

Providing information resets the expected experience for the buyer. Consider the black turtleneck you purchased online, the one that was promised to arrive within seven days. If the package is delayed, you are dissatisfied. If the package is delayed, but you are informed of the delay in advance and perhaps even given a $10 credit off your next purchase, your expectations are reset, and you are satisfied. The provision of information can turn a negative experience into a positive one.

In the bygone days of bricks and mortar, your competitors were reasonably localized. Geography was a barrier to competition. In a digital world, your competition is always in the next tab. Your potential customer can choose you with close to zero real effort—walking from shop to shop on London's Kings Road requires far more effort than starting another Google search. In a world where defecting to a different brand takes zero effort, the investment that you make in setting up the mechanics of brand loyalty is akin to tactics for survival in the modern digital jungle.

How We Think We Buy

The traditional marketing model for how most consumer purchasing decisions are made is described as four steps:

1. Stimulus: We are made aware that mayonnaise is something we can no longer live without.
2. First Moment of Truth (FMOT): We pop down to the store and find the mayonnaise aisle. We look at the 187 different options of mayonnaise and make a decision about which to buy.
3. Moment of Truth (MOT): We choose and purchase a brand of mayonnaise.
4. Second Moment of Truth (SMOT): Our experience with the mayonnaise we chose—was it delicious? Did it live up to the promise made by the brand? (Figure 1.8).

This model was revised in 2011 by Google's Jim Lecinski, who introduced the idea of Zero Moment of Truth (ZMOT). ZMOT is our consumption of the past experiences of others through reviews, recommendations, and Internet-based research. With the addition of ZMOT, the typical process for how we make buying decisions now looks like this:

1. Stimulus: We are made aware that mayonnaise is something we can no longer live without.

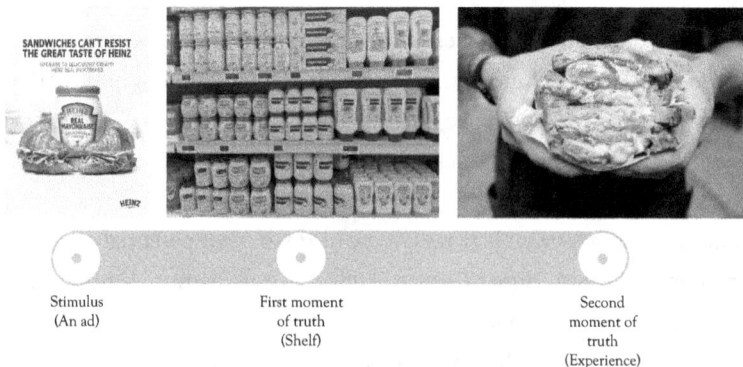

| Stimulus (An ad) | First moment of truth (Shelf) | Second moment of truth (Experience) |

Figure 1.8 The traditional model of how we buy

2. Zero Moment of Truth (ZMOT): We hop onto Facebook and ask our people about their favorite mayonnaise experiences.

3. First Moment of Truth (FMOT): We pop down to the store and find the mayonnaise aisle. We look at the 187 different options of mayonnaise and make a decision about which to buy.

4. Moment of Truth (MOT): We choose and purchase a brand of mayonnaise.

5. Second Moment of Truth (SMOT): Our experience with the mayonnaise we chose—was it delicious? Did it live up to the promise made by the brand?

6. The next person's ZMOT: We post a photo of our epic hot and spicy chicken mayo sandwich on Instagram and rave about how the magic was in the mayo. The review is read by the next person, who is now left wondering how they can live without mayonnaise (Figure 1.9).

This buying process holds for all types of buying, not only for consumer goods or B2C. In commercial or industrial buying, or B2B, the process is described with slightly different words, but it is essentially the same (Figure 1.10):

1. Discovery (Stimulus)
2. Research (ZMOT)

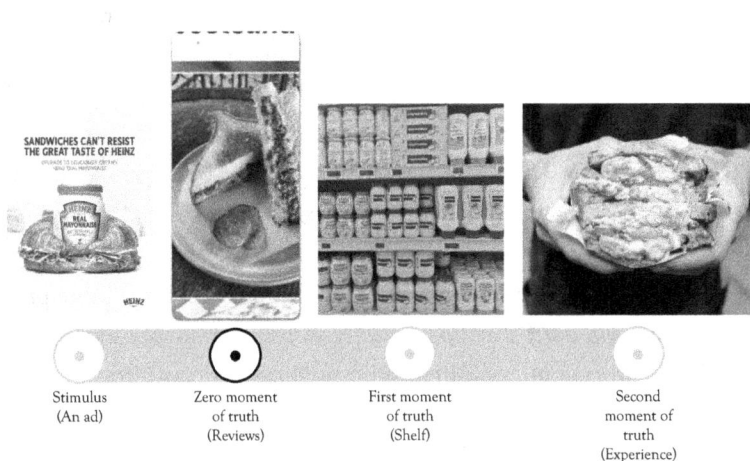

Figure 1.9 *How ZMOT affects the traditional buying model*

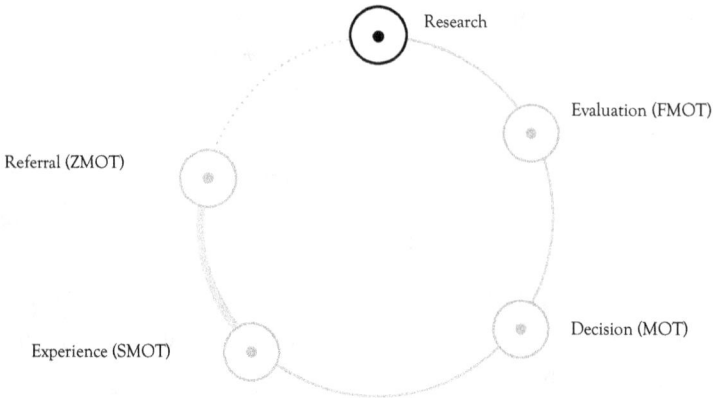

Figure 1.10 The stages of buying correspond to the stages of experience, and the progression of the relationship between buyer and brand

3. Evaluation (FMOT)
4. Decision (MOT)
5. Experience (SMOT)
6. Referral (ZMOT)

The stages in the buying process correspond to the various types of experience. The objective experience or discovery (stimulus) is the starting point in the process. It is your offering to the market. The prior experience of other buyers (ZMOT), whether through direct referral or recommendations of others, influence your research and evaluation phases (ZMOT and FMOT), and set up your expectations. Your experience of the offering (SMOT), layered on your expectations (MOT), results in either positive or negative satisfaction. Your satisfaction affects what you tell others about the brand (ZMOT). And so on, the mechanics of brand loyalty turn the flywheel once more.

Although consumer and enterprise buyers go through the same process, the process itself can take notably different amounts of time to complete. For example, the process of realizing you can't live without mayonnaise, to adding Best Foods Real Mayonnaise to your shopping cart can be completed in 20 seconds, while the process of deciding on which marketing analytics software as a service (SaaS) provider to choose for your growing business could take months. In industrial and enterprise procurement processes, the buying process could take years.

While time scales are important to how you manage and evolve the relationship with your potential customer in a digital space, the steps that your buyer will go through are consistent across industries, as is the degree of influence of ZMOT. Before the massive shift to online buying in 2020, Google reported that over 84 percent of all purchases begin online and that the strength of influence is extremely high across unexpected sectors including automotive, insurance, banking, credit card, travel and (as Cambridge Analytica showed us) even politics (Figure 1.11).

At the heart of the buying process is the decision, or MOT. When we are in the seller's shoes, we tend to assume that this moment is a moment of pure rational thought. We see evidence of this in products and services that try to convince us of their value by focusing on their features. As reasonable and objective as this approach is, we tend to forget that we evaluate things subjectively and often irrationally as soon as we are standing in the buyer's shoes.

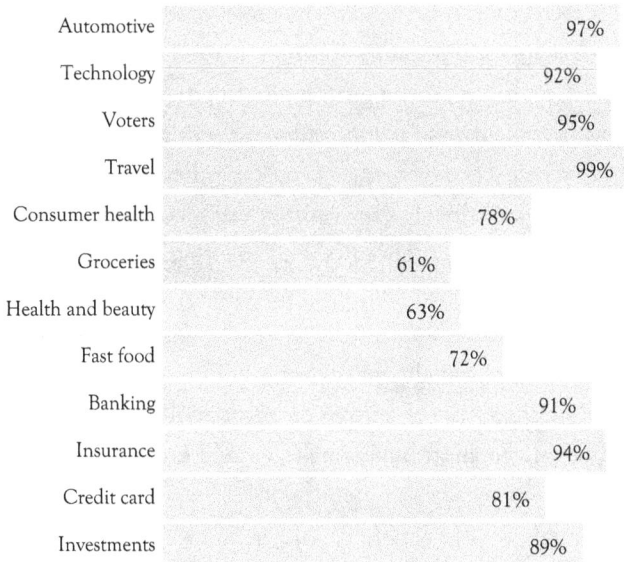

Industry	Strength
Automotive	97%
Technology	92%
Voters	95%
Travel	99%
Consumer health	78%
Groceries	61%
Health and beauty	63%
Fast food	72%
Banking	91%
Insurance	94%
Credit card	81%
Investments	89%

Figure 1.11 Strength of influence of ZMOT across different industries

How We Actually Buy

We may wish human beings were more rational, but our brains, created for a different time and place, get in the way.
—Harvard Business Review, 1998

The headline of my current issue of *Harvard Business Review* reads "How to Change Anyone's Mind" (*Harvard Business Review* 2021). It describes techniques that various colleagues used to persuade Steve Jobs to change his mind on decisions that had global impact, such as the development of the iPhone and App Store, audio streaming, and what eventually became the Apple TV. The techniques gently walked or persuaded Jobs from the edge of "Who the f--- would ever want this" to "Great idea, let's build it." In theory, Steve Jobs made his decisions objectively, rationally evaluating the pros and cons of each situation. In practice, Steve Jobs made decisions only when he felt that the idea was his to begin with. The genius of his colleagues was that they recognized this.

According to conventional economic theory, there is a base assumption that decisions are made rationally and that markets are driven by the interplay of supply and demand. In purely economic terms, we rationally establish a need and fill the need by buying a product for a price set by the forces of supply and demand—a thing we need for a price that is fair. Like Einstein, and anyone who owns more than one pair of shoes will tell you: in practice, theory and practice are not the same.

This discrepancy between what people say they do, what they theoretically should do and what they actually do is loosely what researchers have dubbed "behavioral economics" and "the psychology of persuasion" (Samson 2017; Ashraf, Camerer, and Loewenstein 2005; Cialdini 2006). The patterns that have emerged from these research fields provide crucial insights into how we actually make decisions during the buying process. Understanding the forces of persuasion and deviations from pure rationality can help us to affect buying behavior and evolve the digital brand relationship systematically and predictably.

We Make Decisions to Buy in Predictable and Irrational Ways

In the 1980s, Robert Cialdini took a gap year to work as a door-to-door vacuum cleaner salesman, a used car salesman, and a host of other "unscrupulous" sales positions to figure out how it is that we are influenced to do things that we sometimes do not want to do. His work on influence remains one of the most (pardon the pun) influential books in understanding how we make decisions (Cialdini 2006). Some 30 years later, Dan Ariely shone the light on the consistent and predictable ways in which we, like Steve Jobs, are irrational in our decision making (Ariely 2010). Until this time, and the earlier work of Daniel Kahneman (Kahneman 2013), the standard view was that we are rational in our decision making. Ariely made mainstream knowledge of the predictable patterns to our irrationality.

Together, the principles of influence and patterns of irrationality give us a sound, theoretical lens through which we can understand how it is that we make decisions when we buy. The power of these forces is that they are biologically hardwired into our DNA (Nicholson 1998). They are reliable, slow-moving signals that we can use to predict human buying behaviors in the future because, as the science has shown, even when we understand the errors in our decision-making processes, we continue to repeat the "faulty" behavior. Our reflexive response is to oblige to the faults—and we oblige for reasons that are also hardwired into our brains.

Research shows that our brains are wired to preserve energy (Markman 2015). Making decisions is hard, as it consumes energy. It is almost a matter of survival that we have a strong bias toward taking shortcuts in our decision making. In the last 100 years, the human brain has not changed from an evolutionary perspective. However, the amount of data that we are charged with processing has increased exponentially. Today, a regular person in a Western industrialized nation makes around 35,000 decisions every day (Krockow 2018). From the moment we open our eyes, we're making decisions. These principles of influence and patterns of irrationality are so powerful as they give our brains much-needed shortcuts to making decisions.

Understanding these patterns gives us the foundation from which to create digital artifacts that will encourage a relationship to develop between the newly arrived site visitor and your brand—and the confidence to know that what you create will work, every time, in every industry, with every type of product, service, offering, or experience that you want to sell. Understanding these behavioral patterns will give you an edge in optimizing your digital footprint if used authentically. These patterns are not an invitation, or recipe, for manipulating or cheating the buyer—buyers are too informed and savvy to be made a fool of for long. A deceitful quick win will ultimately result in long-term damage to your brand (*Harvard Business Review* 2020). Use these tools to create a better digital relationship, not to deceive.

Authority: We Shortcut Decision Making by Deferring to Credible Authorities

Our human brains are wired to respond to authority (Cialdini 2006). Consider two factually similar arguments:

1. According to leading evolutionary psychologist Professor Nicholson, our proclivity to look to authority is part of our biogenetic destiny (Nicholson 1998).
2. I'm not an anthropologist, but I bet this hardwired deference to authority dates back to survival in primitive cultural settings.

It is not rocket science to intuit which of the above statements will be more effective in influencing your views. Today, credibility is less about survival and more about energy preservation. Our deference to credibility provides a "shortcut" to making a decision. Connecting our claims to higher authorities, such as the *Harvard Business Review*, or Gartner Research, The Academy Awards, Rotten Tomatoes, TripAdvisor, and using our work-endowed titles and roles, are all instant ways to gain the trust of your audience.

An endorsement by a higher authority eliminates the need to consciously weigh up the evidence and make the decision from first principles. Many successful value propositions lean on credibility from an authority: "Train, Eat and Live better with Chris Hemsworth's team" is compelling, not because Chris Hemsworth has a PhD in nutrition or sports physiology, but because he is seen as an authority. The fact that he's an authority in an unrelated space does not matter that much—in fact, the emergence and growth of "influencer marketing" as a discipline is based on our proclivity to defer our decision making to a famous or credible authority.

Social Proof: We Shortcut Decision Making by Leaning on the Opinions of Others

We are intrinsically wired to mimic the behavior of others (Nicholson 1998): "41 percent of the web is built on WordPress. More bloggers, small businesses, and Fortune 500 companies use WordPress than all other options combined. Join the millions of people that call WordPress. com home" makes a compelling claim that is hard to ignore—would you take the risk of choosing a different platform when 41 percent of your peers have chosen WordPress? Our sense of what is the right thing is based on what others think is the right thing.

> *The most powerful impetus to buy is someone else's advocacy.*
> —*Harvard Business Review,* 2010

We ingest and respond to social proof unconsciously and often rely on it as a shortcut to making decisions (Cialdini 2006). TripAdvisor star ratings are a handy shortcut to the opinions of others at a glance; ditto for product ratings on Amazon, eBay, or your favorite online store. Slogans like "4 out of 5 dentists recommend" were incredibly successful in activating our innate response of falling in line because others do. In the context of hectic lives and decision overloaded days, star ratings provide us with the social proof to make a confident decision easily.

Relative Value: We Shortcut Decision Making by Making Relative, Not Absolute, Comparisons of Value

Let's say you are looking for accommodation for your next holiday. You look on Airbnb, or Booking.com, select your dates, and location click search. You use the resulting list of accommodations, subconsciously, as a "closed world" of choices against which you make comparisons to find the "right" choice. As we don't have an inherent sense of the value of things, we assess what is reasonable by looking at things in relation to other, similar things. In the list of accommodation, you will likely quickly narrow by removing the outliers and compare the rest of the contenders against each other.

In marketing terms, our human propensity to make decisions through comparison gives rise to what is known as "the decoy effect." The decoy effect is a deliberate strategy to present a number of options to the buyer, some of which are deliberately unfavorable, in a move to steer them toward choosing the option which is best for the seller. *The Economist* famously used this strategy when they first released their digital subscriptions, offering consumers three options:

- Option 1: Print version for $59/year
- Option 2: Digital version for $125/year
- Option 3: Print + Digital for $125/year

The second option, the decoy, worked to perfectly steer buyers to purchasing what the magazine wanted them to choose (option 3) and making the consumer feel like they chose the best value option!

It may seem that the introduction of a decoy is a little trivial, but consider the power of that decoy option again. Imagine if the magazine only presented you with two choices:

- Option 1: Print version for $59/year
- Option 2: Print + Digital for $125/year

The decision about which to choose, given these two choices, is infinitely harder, even when you know that option 2 was what you chose in the first scenario.

This principle can also be used successfully when bringing a product or offering to a market with no real competitors. In another famous case, Williams-Sonoma launched a new bread maker to the market at a price point of $275. At the time, it was the only product of its kind on the shelves at Walmart—resulting in lackluster sales as consumers eyed the bread maker with suspicion. The company introduced a comparable: a higher-featured version of the same product at double the price, and sales of the original bread maker took off. The decoy competitor provided the basis for making our irrational comparison-based decision.

Anchoring: We Shortcut Decision Making by Being Anchored to Our First Time

The first time we are exposed to a price for goods or services forms an anchor in our minds that is hard to shift from, even with the passage of time. The anchor creates a benchmark against which all future comparisons are made (Ariely 2010). It is a habit that you likely practice every day: when you buy a coffee without questioning why you are paying $4.50 for something that would make the seller a profit if sold for $1.00, or when you think about buying your next house in a particular neighborhood. Anchoring is particularly evident when the context for our decision changes, but our expectations of what is reasonable do not follow suit. For example, if you move from one city to another, you are at first anchored to the prices in your old town, making all the houses in the new area either seem extremely cheap or extremely expensive. If you sold your home in California for $1.2 million and are in the market for a $350,000 house in Las Vegas, you a far more likely to spend more at an auction than a local Las Vegan, simply because your reasonable price anchor is still set to your old context.

Anchoring is particularly visible when looking at the price sensitivity across generations. We have all heard our grandparents tell the story of "back in my day milk was $0.10 and a loaf of bread nothing over $0.20. Prices these days!" The predictable eye-roll is a reaction to the fact that your generation is anchored to a different normal price point. This chink in our thinking is notable when considering how to position your product both in relation to existing products and with regard to your target audience's age.

Scarcity: We Shortcut Decision Making by Wanting It More When We Can't Have It

It is human nature to want what we can't have. The principle of scarcity goes further and shows us that we are more afraid of losing something than enticed by gaining something of equal value (Cialdini 2006; Ariely 2010). Correspondingly, we are willing to pay more for something that we think is scarce or limited—a fact exploited by every rug business on the planet that has been in its "Final Closing Down 89 percent Off" sale consistently for the last five years.

Our scarcity instinct is accelerated when we are faced with a sudden decrease in availability. The toilet paper shortage during the outbreak of the COVID pandemic is a terrific example, both of social proof and scarcity in action (Labad, González-Rodríguez, Cobo, Puntí and Farré 2021). It is a surprise that no one stopped to consider that this virus placed no extra demands on the need for toilet paper for the average citizen. The power of hardwired behavioral responses in action.

Closely related to the principle of scarcity is the common irrationality we display toward things that we have ownership, or perceived ownership, over (Ariely 2010). Signing up for a free trial of a product or test-driving a new car for the weekend allows you to "pretend" that you own the product. This act of virtual ownership is enough to trick us into feeling a sense of loss when the trial period ends, or the car is returned—and even though the thing was never ours when it is gone, we mourn as though it had been.

Take note of times when you feel the pull of signing up to a limited time, free one month only access to the new gym opening up in your neighborhood. Even as a person who thinks deeply about this stuff daily, I find myself reactive to the same formula: true story, I did indeed sign up to the limited time, free one month only access to the new gym opening up in my neighborhood next month. You probably did the same at some point too—as will your buyers when you set these forces in motion.

Free: We Shortcut Decision Making by Wanting It More When It Is Free

Along with scarcity driving us to desire something more, the price tag of *free* has the power to send us into a similar irrational frenzy (Ariely 2010). Let's say you have a choice of paying $2.50 for your regular Barista made coffee or $0.50 for an instant coffee from the 7-11. Using standard economic analysis, you would do a quick cost–benefit calculation and decide to buy the Barista coffee as it is a far superior product for a great price. Now, if the price of both items were reduced by $0.50, making your Barista coffee $2.00 and the instant coffee *free*, economic rationality dictates that your choice should remain the same. In reality, most people choose the instant coffee with the price tag of *free*.

The power of free comes from the fact that it is the price point at which all risk is eliminated. Free carries with it no downside in economic terms. You, and I, have at some stage in life come home with a suitcase filled with conference loot (no, I did not need seven plastic drink bottles with the Salesforce logo emblazoned on them, or individually wrapped bars of hotel soap, which forever lie stockpiled at the back of the bathroom drawer). We took those items because there was no downside to doing so, not because there was a need or an upside. We took those items because our biological predecessors would have done the same: a life on the edge meant that even a tiny loss could jeopardize existence, hardwiring a preference for limiting the downside into our human DNA (Nicholson 1998).

Consistency: We Shortcut Decision Making by Striving to Remain Consistent, Even When Going against Ourselves

Once we take a stand, we have an almost obsessive propensity to remain consistent with our stated position (Cialdini 2006). In a study of homeowners in California, it was shown that those who were willing to have a small billboard placed in their front yard were far more likely to accept a larger, unsightly billboard than those who were not prewarned. The principle of consistency is used extensively as a strategy by telemarketers to keep you talking, walking you from the point of never having spoken to this person, or having considered installing solar panels on your roof to booking an appointment. Consistency is effectively the legendary urban myth of the frog in boiling water, only it is true.

If the deltas are small enough, you can find yourself remaining consistent with your perspective and ending up in a place you never intended to. This strategy is used successfully in hostage negotiations (Voss 2016). To win the confidence of the perpetrator, a skilled negotiator can move the hostage from a hostile position to a position of standing down by incrementally laying stepping stones that the perpetrator is biologically wired to continue stepping onto. Each step elicits a "yes, that's right, that's consistent with what I just said" from the perpetrator, making it almost impossible for them to reverse out due to the forces of the consistency principle.

In the context of buying goods, we fall prey to this strategy often unsuspectingly. We walk into a nice shop and start a conversation with the salesperson. The salesperson shows us a lovely dress. The dress is way more expensive than we ever intended, and not even something that we need. The salesperson says it looks great on us. We look in the mirror and agree, "yes, that's right, it does look great on me." On the way out, we buy a pair of earrings too because they do look fabulous with the dress we never intended to buy. This familiar pattern is replicated in the digital space so often that we may not notice it anymore. At checkout, we are presented with the option to take advantage of free shipping if we spend another $32.49. We have already committed to buying the first item and so willingly add one more to get the free shipping. The power of free plus consistency deals us an irresistible double whammy.

Inertia: We Shortcut Decision Making by Preferring To Do ... Nothing

I work with companies who are looking to expand into new markets or unlock new revenue opportunities in existing markets. Quite often, these are companies that have maximized their market share in a particular market, and now seek to expand into the next market. Part of the process involves looking at the competitive landscape and an analysis of the points of difference. This analysis typically produces a matrix of features versus competitors and a bunch of ticks and crosses. Rationally, the buyer would look at such a grid and choose the provider with the most ticks.

Many businessowners think that success follows if they can show that their offering scores the most ticks. That simply having superior features, or a lower price, or both, will activate their target audience to make the switch to their brand. If their target customer is using a competitors' services, no problem, they will leave their current provider in preference of their demonstrated and superior offering—another example where the practice and the theory do not align in reality.

In reality, the inertia of doing nothing is stronger than the potential upside, even if the upside is risk-free. Jonah Berger describes this beautifully, showing us that the certainty of today wins over the uncertainty of tomorrow (Berger 2020). The act of doing nothing wins over changing to your brand, regardless of how many more features your product has.

Your competitor list, therefore, includes inaction. To counteract inaction and get anyone to choose your brand, you must remove all the obstacles to render the desired behavior easy.

Recall that behind every single potential buyer, there is a human being who is juggling soccer drop-offs, aspirations for promotions, the desire for an occasional mid-week date, fleeting hopes of fitness, and 35,000 decisions every day. The evaluation of your product, service, or innovative offering is one more thing in their day. It is the only thing in your day. Creating conditions that trigger reflexive, biologically wired responses in decision making preserve energy. Putting in place artifacts to de-risk the unknowns of tomorrow preserve energy. Crafting active participation in the buying journey conserves energy and starts developing a sense of loss even before the purchase decision is made.

Decision Shortcuts Shorten the Buying Process

In research reported in the *Harvard Business Review* (Edelman 2010), the authors found that the traditional buying process (discover, evaluate, research, decide, experience) is cut down to only two steps (decide and experience) when a trusted source recommends the product or service. The prior collective experience of others not only influences the next buyer, but it fast tracks that buyer into choosing your brand.

Decide and buy. Decide and buy. The relationship you form with the next buyer reduces the buying process for future buyers from five steps to two (decide: MOT and experience: SMOT). A good relationship with your brand removes 60 percent of the obstacles that need to be overcome to make your brand the chosen one. The only thing that remains is to ensure that your next buyer falls in love with your offering (Figure 1.12).

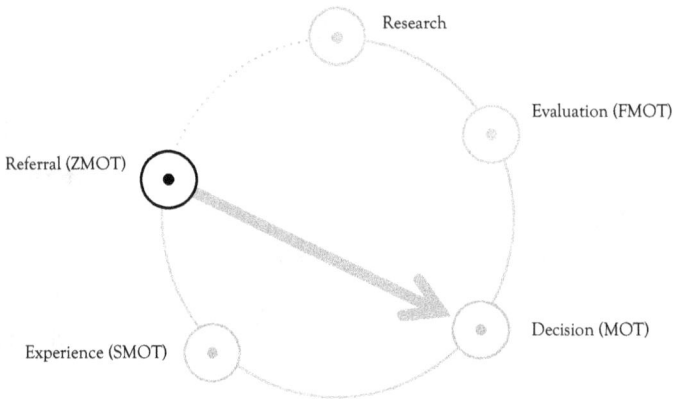

Figure 1.12 Decision shortcuts and referrals from trusted sources shorten the buying process

We Fall in Love in Predictable and Irrational Ways

In the late 1990s, psychologist Arthur Aron and a team of researchers published a process that, when applied, could make two complete strangers fall in love (Aron, Melinat, Aron, Vallone and Bator 1997). *The Experimental Generation of Interpersonal Closeness* presented a set of 36 questions, which, if asked in the order prescribed, guaranteed the transition from stranger to love interest by the end of the session. This somewhat outlandish science was famously put to the test by a skeptical journalist from the *New York Times*, who applied the formula and—unexpectedly—found love (Len Catron 2015).

It turns out that the process for creating a deep relationship between two strangers can be applied to creating a relationship between a stranger and your brand. The 36 questions are not magical. Many are the types of questions that you would naturally ask when getting to know someone. "Given the choice of anyone in the world, whom would you want as a dinner guest" or "For what in your life do you feel most grateful?" are pretty standard conversational fare. The absolute breakthrough in Aron's approach is the discovery that a critical element in the development of a close relationship is "sustained, escalating, reciprocal, personal self-disclosure." If you look at the questions again, you'll see that the order in which they are presented progressively "squeezes" the two strangers together by asking questions in an order that slowly escalates their intimacy, yet does it at a tempo that does not scare them off. As early as question eight, the couple is asked to "name three things that you and your partner have in common." Both the language used (your partner) and the question (list things you have in common) is an enormous leap in the traditional cadence of conversations between strangers, even if considering two strangers conversing with the intent of romance, such as a first date (Figure 1.13).

Aron's formula for love is a perfect application of Cialdini's principle of consistency: the two strangers start with innocuous, simple questions, and with slowly increasing velocity, are thrust into a very intimate space from which they are not biologically designed to backtrack. The process of falling in love triggers our hardwired reflexes of irrationality and influence. And it works beautifully.

This book, of course, is not about traditional romance between two strangers. It is about creating romance, or the conditions for "love" between a stranger (your site visitor) and your brand. The playbook for love between strangers is valuable and applicable in this context, primarily because the person falling in love is, in fact, a person. That they are falling in love with an intangible concept like a brand is inconsequential—the process, the emotions, the actions taken, and commitments made are the

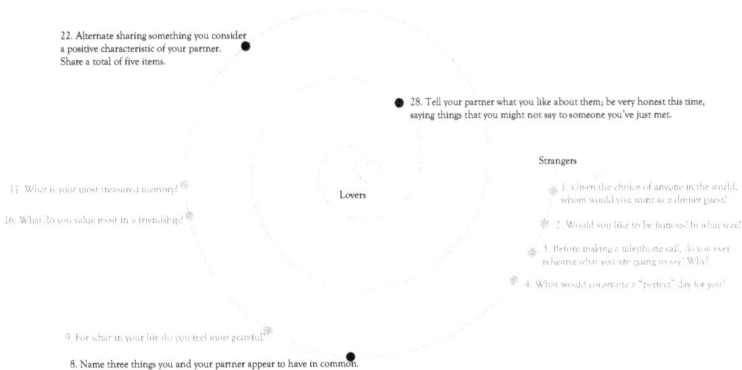

Figure 1.13 The thirty-six love questions generate a cadence of increasing closeness: note the way that fairly benign questions are interspersed with more vulnerable ones and how the tension immediately after a vulnerable question eases off in the next one

same. Almost a decade ago, Spike Jonze's movie *Her* challenged us to imagine whether we could have feelings for something that was "not real." If you rewatch the same film today, only 10 years on, the concepts in the film are not nearly as far-fetched.

The idea that you can fall in love with a brand is unquestionably true today. Evidence exists at every fashion show, in every tech workspace, at every large sporting event, and in every shopping center food hall. The recipe for how to create increasing commitment and affection for your brand is described in Part II. Like the formula for real love, if done right, the process will trigger deep-rooted biological responses, almost guaranteeing success.

We Spend Our Marketing Budgets in Predictable and Irrational Ways

The marketing industry has done a stellar job of marketing the success of their own poor performance. They have conditioned us to accept that industry average conversion rates are in the order of 1 to 5 percent (Kim 2021). Consider this excerpt from Kim's article, entitled "What's a Good Conversion Rate? (It's Higher Than You Think)":

> Across industries, the average landing page conversion rate was 2.35%, yet the top 25% are converting at 5.31% or higher. Ideally, you want to break into the top 10%—these are the landing pages with conversion rates of 11.45% or higher.

Let's assume that your marketing team is brilliant, and you routinely achieve conversion rates of 11.45 percent. If your typical conversion rates are 11.45 percent, then you are, in effect, accepting that 88.55 percent of your total marketing budget is wasted. If you are at the more typical end of the spectrum, you have been conditioned to think that zero returns on 97.65 percent of your marketing dollars are an outcome to be celebrated. Other than the casino industry, modern marketing is the only industry I know of where losing 97.65 percent of your money is considered a terrific investment (Figure 1.14).

In the olden days, businesses would pay pennies for Google Ads clicks. In those days, the economics made sense. Today, Google is smarter, and

Google ads seo	$690.40
Seo for roofing	$123.93
Website grader hubspot	$73.57
Local search marketing	$13.93
Workers comp lawyer near me	$171.32
Car crash lawyers	$135.86
Car accident lawyer	$112.34
Midlife crisis men	$2.76
Pontoon repair	$7.12

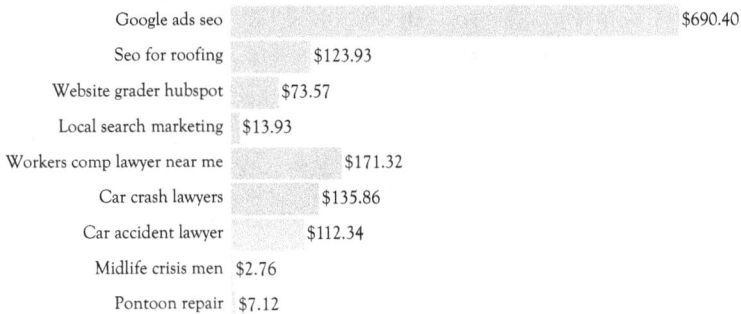

Figure 1.14 The cost of Google Adwords is based on popularity and competition: popular keywords in industries with deeper pockets can be hundreds of dollars per click

the Google Ads pricing model is directly linked to demand and capacity. If you are buying keywords in medicine, SEO, or legal fields, your cost per click can be hundreds of dollars; if you are buying keywords that are not often searched for, such as pontoon repair or mid-life crisis, your cost per click may be a few dollars a click (Schewan 2021). For example, a topic like "google ads SEO" can cost between $13 and $690 per click. So, if you are a mid-sized digital marketing agency wanting to advertise your expertise with "google ads SEO," a monthly budget of $10,000 would allow for around 30 clicks at an average cost of $350 per click. Of the 30 clicks, if we assume that your conversion rates are at the high end of market averages, say 5.31 percent, you may get as many as 1.6 customers signing up to your services. You would need to make over $6,250 per customer per month simply to break even.

Google Ads revenue has been increasing year on year. Between 2018 and 2019, Google made an additional $18.35 billion from advertising revenue (Johnson 2021). To put that in context—the increase in revenue for the 2018 to 2019 financial year for Google was around the size of the GDP of many countries in Africa.

Google Ads are generating more revenue for the company each year because Google is solving for Google's mission, not for the mission of your business (Harrison 2021). To this end, there is a tremendous incentive for things like "organic" search results to be throttled and results from more "reputable sources" to be given a leg up. This trend is not particular or limited to Google. Like Google, Facebook's ad revenue is growing at around 17 percent per year. In 2019 to 2020, Facebook reported an additional $13.56 billion from advertising revenue.

It is most likely not a coincidence that the increase in Facebook's advertising revenue coincides with changes to the feed algorithm, which decreases the organic reach of posts. If you are a business with 10,000 followers, it's likely that only 650 of your fans will see one of your posts. According to Hubspot, Facebook reports that "you should assume organic reach will eventually arrive at zero." Once again, there is strong evidence to suggest that Facebook is solving for its own mission, not the mission of your business.

Following the money flows, we can make the fair prediction that Google, Facebook, Instagram, or YouTube (insert your favorite social media platform) are solving for their own business models, which includes creating new ways to squeeze more advertising dollars out of your business. Coupled with recent changes in the name of data privacy, restrictions on how cookies are handled at the operating system level has the potential to render strategies based on adwords far less effective than the current industry averages. According to Google's research, most publishers could lose 50 to 70 percent of their revenue if they don't reconfigure their approach to advertising and data management by 2022.

The future is not random—the way you spend your marketing dollars, the strategy you have for creating long term, recession-proof revenue streams needs your immediate attention. The signals are all here now. Schwartz could see them back in 1997: "Marketers should not be on the web for exposure, they should be on the web for results." Retention is the new acquisition.

How do you get retention? Excellent that you asked.

Summary: The Formula for Digital Brand Romance

The creation of an excellent digital brand relationship can be scripted. Spending decades working with brands worldwide and researching buying behavior as it manifests in technology, psychology, and behavioral economics has led me to discover six critical moments in the customer journey, from first contact with a brand to ultimate brand loyalty and advocacy.

In Part II, you will learn the script or process for digital brand romance: the ADORE process™. The ADORE process™ has been tested with brands in a wide range of industries: from edible seaweed to restaurant booking platforms, architectural timber producers, fintech apps, construction SaaS systems, accounting, technology, old fashioned engineering firms and modern marketing agencies. Consistently, the brands that apply the ADORE process™ realize above-average conversions, significantly increased retentions, and higher and accelerated sales rates. When you understand the basis of ADORE, you will be able to spot and resolve issues in the digital artifacts that define your relationships with buyers. This will allow you to optimize your website, e-mail marketing campaigns, apps, and e-commerce stores for lasting and meaningful relationships that transcend individual transactions.

PART II

The ADORE Process

In Part I, we examined the factors that conspire to influence the buying process and looked at the macro and micro signals to make reasonable predictions about the new normal in commerce. We deduced that in order to future-proof your business growth, you would need to shift your marketing strategy from transactional to emotional. We noted that emotional engagement is required to build strong and lasting relationships between your buyers and your brand, and that these relationships begin online.

In a world of fast and constant change, relationships that boost loyalty and advocacy are your tools for conquering tomorrow's unknowns. A lasting relationship between the buyer and the brand is increasingly valued, so much so that the relationship and experience with your brand is indistinguishable from the products and services you offer.

> *When the customer journey is crafted just right, the process becomes the product.*
>
> —Alexander Manu, 2017

In this chapter, you will learn the ADORE process™ for creating lasting relationships in a digital space. You will learn simple, objective tactics to recognize moments of relationship breakdown and learn strategies to turn these moments around.

For consistency, we will assume that your website is the primary location where the relationship between your buyer and brand evolves. If your business does not have a website, and instead relies on social media platforms or in-app purchasing, don't worry—the same ADORE process™ applies to most digital artifacts, including websites, apps, e-mail marketing campaigns, and social media platforms. In this case, simply replace "website" with "app" or similar as you read. We will expand on how you can apply the ADORE process™ to optimize experiences in other channels in Part III.

Your website is one of the most important digital artifacts, and according to Google Research, the stickiest of touchpoints throughout the customer journey. Applying the ADORE process™ is proven to increase conversion rates by optimizing the customer journey from the very first touch on your website, all the way through to recommendations, repeat buys, and learnings from those who leave you. The power of the ADORE process™ is that it is objective, repeatable, and therefore consistent in its results—you can apply ADORE to any sales and marketing funnel and get the same insights and benefits each time.

Like most businesses, you are already collecting marketing data. In some cases, you may have assembled a team that uses this data to tune your marketing and sales activity. If this is you, you already know the challenge of finding talent with experience in the technical and data side of marketing—the elusive search engine optimization (SEO) and conversion rate optimization (CRO) unicorn. The ADORE process™ provides the unicorn for you, empowering your marketing team with the data analysis skills that typically fall outside their core passion and capability. ADORE makes the insights available to your entire team, empowering them to effectively use the data you are collecting. The ADORE process™ gives you a consistent approach to deploying experiments and rolling out changes—without compromising the relationship with your customers or stifling innovation and creativity in your organization.

> *Our success at Amazon is a function of how many experiments we do per year, per month, per week, per day.*
>
> —Jeff Bezos, CEO Amazon

The ADORE process™ will help you pinpoint inefficiencies, provide insights into what may be causing issues, and show you common approaches to resolving these issues. The net result is that you will have a systematic way to ensure that your most important digital asset is optimized—giving you the best possible chance of converting more site visitors into loyal brand advocates.

An Overview of the ADORE Process™

The ADORE process™ consists of the following core milestones in the customer journey (Figure 2.1):

1. Zero Seconds: The Arrival
2. Ten Seconds: The First Impression
3. Three Minutes: The First Date
4. Sign-up: The Honeymoon
5. First 48 Hours: The Reality
6. Upgrade: The Moment of Truth
7. Recommend, or RIP

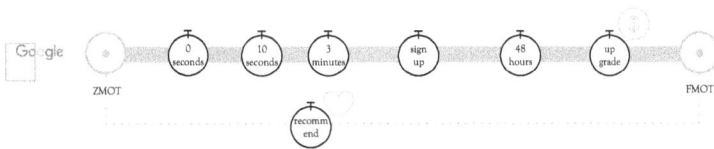

Figure 2.1 The ADORE process™ for digital brand loyalty

Anxieties

Your new site visitor arrives at your website in the context of their regular day. They are on your website because they are looking to solve a particular challenge in their own life. They arrive at your website preloaded with anxieties, inertia, and the distractions of 35,000 decisions a day. They do not arrive at your website in a vacuum—your job, in order to create a lasting relationship with the stranger on your doorstep, is to successively remove any anxieties or blockers that they may have and to do this in advance of them noting that they have the anxiety in the first place.

Ten Seconds: Does It Feel Right?

Your potential customers assess whether you are in the running for their attention in the first ten seconds or less. You have this long to establish credibility and appeal to their intuitive response to "does this feel right for me." Inward and unclear messaging will not only lose a prospect, but it could also lead to them buying elsewhere and spending more with your competitors.

Three Minutes: Why Should I Stay?

If you captured their attention in the first instance, you will have the privilege of unfolding the storyline of how your product makes their life better. You have at most three minutes to do this, so leveraging terrific customer testimonials and articulating your offerings in crisp, customer-centric ways are key. Feelings of confusion, lack of trust, and lack of clarity will impact your potential customer pool.

Sign-Up: Should I Play with It?

You have done the hard work and steered the customer through the virtual door. This phase is critical to get right, and if you do, you stand a chance of creating a loyal fan, and with that, increased revenue. Poorly packaged products and out of sync pricing models are the most common causes of low conversion rates.

First 48 Hours: Can I Make It Work for Me?

The First 48 Hours are critical to establishing ownership and success. Common mistakes at this phase include onboarding that creates too much homework or does not deliver on the promises made earlier in the customer journey. The price of being ineffective in this phase are high churn rates and missed opportunities for conversion to paid and premium products.

Upgrade: Do You Make My Life Better

The ultimate litmus test—did you deliver value? Has your product become part of your customer's regular routine? Low return-usage rates and poor engagement are a red flag that your product is either not delivering or perceived as not delivering on the promise to make your customer's life better. The costs here are higher than lost revenue—the cost is lost future earnings through low loyalty.

Recommend, or RIP

Technically, the Recommend, or RIP milestone falls outside the customer journey under your control on your website, app, e-mail marketing campaign, or social media e-commerce site. This milestone is included in the ADORE formula as it represents the compounding effects of the mechanics of brand loyalty.

How ADORE Fits Into the Buying Process

Recall the typical buying process from Part I of the book. The ADORE process™ optimizes the space between the Zero Moment of Truth (ZMOT) and First Moment of Truth (FMOT) (Figure 2.2). The space between SMOT and FMOT is the only segment in the buying journey that is entirely under your control—you get to decide exactly how to tell your story to each stranger that lands on your website, how to nudge them from first date to full commitment. You get to refine and evolve the relationship with your customers over time: sometimes you will get things very right, and sometimes a website update will set you backward. The objectivity of ADORE will help you to track what to do more of and what to roll back on.

Stimulus   ZMOT   Adore process   FMOT   SMOT

Figure 2.2 How the ADORE process™ fits into the typical buying process

How ADORE Fits Into Existing Sales
and Marketing Frameworks

You are likely already familiar with many marketing and sales funnel frameworks and methodologies. If that is the case, you will be able to easily place the ADORE process™ in the context of your existing mental models (Figure 2.3). Whatever your preferred model, it provides a particular perspective on how to manage each stage of the end-to-end inception, creation, delivery, operations, and maintenance of the customer experience. The ADORE process™ does not compete with these frameworks. It simply provides an extra layer for you to manipulate.

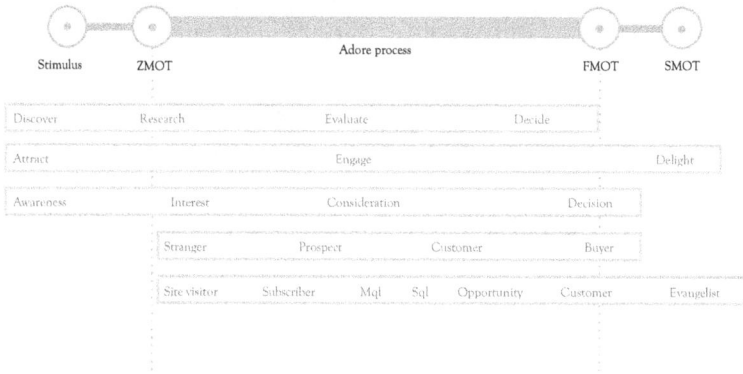

Figure 2.3 How the ADORE process™ fits within traditional marketing and sales frameworks

ADORE is the emotional layer from which the relationship with your brand is constructed. It describes what happens to each human buyer as they transition from stranger through prospect, customer, and on to buyer; or from site visitor to subscriber, marketing qualified lead (MQL), sales qualified lead (SQL), opportunity, customer, and brand evangelist. Placing ADORE in the context of existing frameworks will also help you map the metrics in each milestone to ones that you may already be collecting through marketing automation tools like Hubspot, HotJar, Pardot, or similar.

Summary

The ADORE process™ is based on six critical emotional milestones in the customer journey. Each milestone represents a deepening of commitment between your site visitor and brand, and reflects the evolution of this relationship in the digital space. Like a relationship between two humans, there is a cadence that builds increasing trust and intimacy, which must be respected for the relationship to succeed. This optimal pace of relationship evolution is represented in the ADORE milestone names: Zero Seconds, Ten Seconds, Three Minutes, Sign-up, Upgrade (and Recommend or RIP) (Figure 2.4). The milestones are ordered in a specific way and can't be skipped over—the stranger that landed on your website needs to pass through each milestone sequentially to consummate the relationship with your brand.

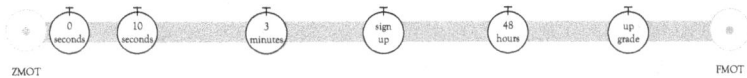

Figure 2.4 Elements of the ADORE process™

In order, the six emotional milestones in the ADORE process™ are as follows:

1. Zero Seconds: The arrival
2. Ten Seconds: Does it feel right?
3. Three Minutes: Why should I stay?
4. Sign-up: Should I play with it?
5. First 48 Hours: Can I make it work for me?
6. Upgrade: Do you make my life better?
7. Recommend or RIP: Do you make me a hero?

Technically, the last milestone—Recommend or RIP—does not happen on your website, so is not within your control. However, as recommendations are a vital component of lasting relationships, we'll explore how to leverage this milestone and use it to create powerful connections between existing and future buyers. Think of this as a bonus seventh step in the ADORE process™.

The remaining chapters in Part II describe each of the ADORE milestones in turn. The sections all follow the same structure, making it easier for you to use this part of the book as a handy reference. Each section is structured as follows:

1. Overview
2. Description of the milestone

3. Anxieties that must be addressed to complete this milestone

4. Common causes of issues

5. How to fix issues

6. How to measure success

7. Case study

8. Summary

The case study in each chapter tells a story of a successful brand that you may have not heard of. Many of the case studies in this book are deliberately not based on brands that are already household names. Instead, they showcase businesses that may be similar to yours—ones embarking on a growth phase to scale their offering globally. Each of the brands profiled applied the ADORE process™ with limited in-house marketing capabilities, leaning on the process itself to achieve the reported results.

Zero Seconds

The Arrival

Introduction

This chapter will show you how to:

1. Drive more traffic to your website
2. Understand potential declines in traffic flow
3. Take action to improve returns on your marketing spend

The relationship between the buyer and the brand begins the moment that they land on your website. At this moment, the Zero Second mark (Figure 2.5), your marketing budget has been entirely exhausted. Whatever efficiencies you can introduce from this point forward in your marketing or sales funnel all translate to pure profit.

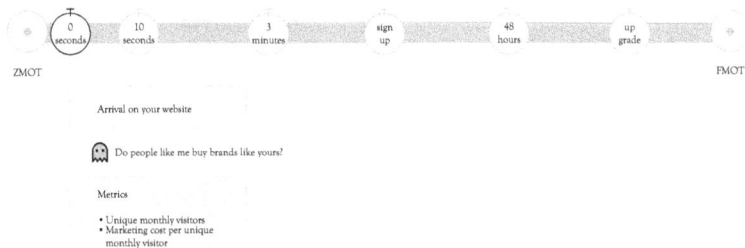

Figure 2.5 The Zero Second milestone of the ADORE process™

The Zero Second milestone is the point of arrival on your website and the gateway to your brand. It is the necessary first step—the mere showing up at the first date. In marketing terms, this moment is typically referred to as search engine optimization (SEO).

Search Engine Optimization

Recall that over 90 percent of all traffic on the Internet originates on page one of Google. SEO has emerged as the specialty field dedicated to the mechanics of "improving the quantity and quality of leads to your website," in other words, how your page ends up on page one of Google. In a broad sense, SEO is the science of predicting which keywords will be typed by your next buyer into Google search when looking for products and services like yours, and ensuring that your website is rewarded with a page one ranking by Google when these keywords are typed in.

> SEO is having the most helpful answer to the question being asked by your future customer.

According to Google's mission, their number one priority is to make sure search results are accurate and relevant. The process by which Google arrives at this mission is opaque, increasingly sophisticated, and changes frequently. The Google algorithms are now clever enough to understand the meaning of a web page and the entities described by it. The old days of stuffing keywords into meta tags and using tools to game the system are ineffective and will even earn you "demerit" points with Google's ranking algorithm.

Attempts to stay on top of Google's algorithm updates are equally futile—according to one of the top SEO experts in the world, Neil Patel, Google changes its page ranking algorithm over 3,000 times a year. An army of developers would struggle to keep up with that. As a result, techniques that drive traffic to your website today can be rendered useless tomorrow.

The escalating cost of AdWords, technology changes by major players like Apple, and the opaque nature of the Google Page Ranking Algorithm make it impossible to predict with certainty what will work best tomorrow. When it comes down to it, SEO is still very much an art and will probably remain so as you and I have no control over the inputs. The best that we can do is optimize for the slow-moving signals and adopt strategies to limit our reliance on AdWords alone.

The Slow-Moving Elements of SEO

There are three reasonably stable elements of SEO that are likely to remain significant inputs into Google's Page Ranking algorithm. These are described below.

Mobile-First Website

Google recently announced that they will penalize websites that are not mobile-first. This change certainly makes sense, as the vast majority of content is now consumed on mobile devices. That said, a large proportion of websites are still not optimized for mobile. This element is nonnegotiable for your business—your Zero Second Moment must work perfectly on mobile devices.

Healthy HTML Structure

Again, this element is nonnegotiable—the HTML code on your website must be well-formed, or you will be penalized by the page rank algorithm. A modern content management system, such as Squarespace, Wix, or WordPress, will usually get you 80 percent there. You can capture the remaining 20 percent by using one of the many web checking tools available.

Relevant and Fresh Content

Websites that deliver new and relevant content will rank higher. The page rank algorithms are sophisticated enough to understand the meaning of your page contents and currently favor content pieces that are over 1,800 words long. Given the commercial landscape, it is likely that YouTube video content (Google owns YouTube) will add favorably to your page ranking scores in the emerging future.

Limiting Reliance on AdWords

Recall from Part I that the economics of Google AdWords are based on demand and what the market sector can bear. For example, suppose your customer acquisition cost (CAC) is more than what the customer will spend in their first transaction with you. In that case, you may want to diversify your reliance on Google AdWords and explore strategies based on nodes, aggregators, or partnerships.

Partnership-based marketing is based on the concept that the partner alliance delivers access to a trusted, recommended audience in exchange for something of value. For example, professional associations, such as the American Medical Association, American Institute of Certified Public Accountants, International Council of Shopping Centres, or the Society of Petroleum Engineers, can serve as useful nodes that can provide access to your target audience at scale. To make the alliance valuable, you need to solve for the association, which, quite typically, is simply providing relevant content to their member constituents. Done right, the members get value from the educational material. The association remains relevant in the eyes of the membership. Your brand gets trusted access to a large cohort of your target audience. You'll need to do the math on this, but there is a good chance that the economics of partner relationships will trump the use of AdWords.

> *We've seen an explosion in growth in the partnership economy… our most mature customers growing revenue in the partnership channel by more than 50 per cent year on year.*
> —Adam Furness, Impact

Whatever strategy works best for your business, once deployed, it will have the effect of delivering a new site visitor to your website. At that very moment, when this stranger steps onto your site, they will arrive preloaded with numerous anxieties. Your job is to preempt and alleviate these anxieties, thereby nudging the site visitor to go on to the next ADORE milestone. Each successive milestone deepens the relationship with your brand.

Anxieties at Zero Seconds

> *What I hate is if you show up and tell me everything is low risk. Don't make me laugh, don't make me feel good. Make me feel scared, and then make me feel comfortable because you're dealing with all the risks.*
> —Thomas Zurbuchen, NASA

It's tempting to think that your customers are unique and that the product or service you have on offer is so much better than anything else out there that your customers will arrive with no anxieties. Instead, they will simply know that you are the one.

Having seen hundreds if not thousands of products, services, and offerings peacocking their wares to prospective buyers, I can unequivocally vouch that every single human that lands on your website will land there with fears. These may be subconscious, they may be unarticulated, but they are there. The anxieties are baked into our human DNA.

At the Zero Second milestone, when a stranger lands on your website, there is one primary anxiety or fear that they will need resolved if they are going to allow you the next ten seconds of their attention, and that is: do people like me buy brands like yours?

If your brand has been recommended by a trusted friend or a credible source like TripAdvisor or Rotten Tomatoes, this anxiety has been resolved before the stranger arrived on your website. In this case, your site visitor is effectively fast-tracked through the Zero Second milestone and straight on to the Ten Second, or even Three Minute, milestone.

Common Causes of Issues

"How do I drive more traffic to my website" is the number one question asked of the Google Insights team. Most of the businesses I work with come to me to answer this question, and while there are times when we will address the issue of volume, these cases are in the minority. For most clients, the real issue is not the volume of traffic but rather inefficiencies downstream, which lead to low conversion rates.

To ascertain whether you have issues at the Zero Second milestone, look for:

1. A drop in your total unique site visitors
2. A spike in your customer complaints
3. A decrease in your Net Promoter Score (NPS)

Declines in Total Unique Site Visitors

The best indicator of issues at the Zero Second milestone is the number of unique site visitors to your website each month. A word of caution here: it is very tempting and easy to get swayed by vanity stats and large numbers—after all, a campaign that delivers 100,000 unique site visitors to your website does sound impressive. The thing to remember, however, is that site visitors are not buyers. Paying to drive traffic to your website without plugging the holes in the funnel downstream chews up your marketing budget without increasing sales.

> Site visitors don't buy. Buyers buy. Create buyers, don't count visitors.

In situations where the site traffic is insufficient, common causes include:

1. No marketing strategy to drive traffic to your website
2. Low ranking on Google
3. A mismatch between words used in the copy of your website, and the words used by your target audience when searching for products and services like yours
4. No system for measuring changes in site traffic, and potential causes of fluctuations
5. A new website update rolled out which breaks prior SEO elements

Increased Customer Complaints or Decreased NPS

Fluctuations in unique site visitor metrics will give you an indication that you have a problem on hand. Customer complaints and NPS declines can be an early predictor of future reductions in site traffic. Triangulate the data with any changes to your product or service, particularly when there has been an unexpected spike or drop in these metrics.

How to Fix Issues

Fixing issues at the Zero Second milestone will increase traffic to your website. Here are common ways that you can improve the flow of visitors to your website.

Create a Simple Marketing Strategy

Start by creating a marketing strategy. Your strategy will be unique to you and needs to consider:

1. The type of business that you operate. Do you rely on high volumes of visitors, or can you achieve your sales targets with a handful of the right people coming to your website?
2. A baseline target for your site visitors. An easy way to get this number is to take an average of unique monthly visitors from your Google Analytics panel. You can use this as a starting point to compare against.
3. Decide whether your primary strategy will rely on paid advertising, such as AdWords, or partnerships and relationships with nodes.
4. Put in place a basic system for deploying and testing marketing strategies. For example, deploying a Google Ads campaign and monitoring traffic in Google Analytics; starting an e-mail marketing campaign and tracking site visitors in MailChimp or Google Analytics; getting an article featured in a credible news site, and tracking clickthroughs in your analytics panel.

Optimize Your Website for SEO Rankings on Google Search

Ensure that you can tick the boxes on the fundamental, slow-moving elements of SEO:

1. Is your website structurally healthy and optimized for mobile? Run a health check using one of the many tools, such as Neil Patel's Site Analyzer or Google's mobile checker.
2. Check whether you are using the right keywords, both on your website and in paid advertising. Tools such as Google's AdWords Planner, Keywords Everywhere, and SEMrush are useful.
3. Research the keywords that your biggest competitors are using and optimize for the same. Tools like SEMrush and Keywords Everywhere allow you to easily research your competitors' sites. Google Trends is another handy place to look for keywords that are in and out of favor with searchers.

Remember to rerun your site checker tools after each website update to ensure that the new changes have not inadvertently broken anything. Note that each tool uses a proprietary scoring system, so a 67 score from Neil Patel is not comparable to a 67 score from SEMrush or another tool. Use the scores as a relative measure, not absolutes. If your score went down, roll back, and figure out what happened, and if your score improved, good work!

Rewrite Your Website Copy in the Language of Your Target Audience

One of the most challenging and most common symptoms that affect your digital presence is the use of inward-focused language in your website copy. It is normal and natural to use language particular to your specific business or domain of expertise. However, these are not necessarily the words that your target customers use when searching for your offering. As a general guide, if you are describing your internal business processes, structures, or using niche terminology, you may be introducing an opportunity not to be found. Using a professional copywriter is highly recommended, as it is often tough to unlearn the language used inside the business and approach your messaging from the perspective of your target audience.

Monitor Site Metrics

Set up a basic system to keep track of your site traffic:

1. Connect your website to Google Analytics
2. Measure unique monthly visitors
3. Record any marketing deployments, changes to paid advertising campaigns, or major website updates (and compare to resulting changes in site traffic) and note the changes in your overall site metrics after these rollouts.

Reach Your Target Audience at Scale Through Nodes

Think of ways to reach your target audience at scale by forming relationships with nodes. Solve for the pain points of the node, for example, remaining relevant to their membership base or delivering fresh and newsworthy content.

How to Measure Success

The following metrics can measure success at the Zero Second milestone:

1. Unique monthly visitors
2. Marketing cost per unique monthly visitor
3. Cost of customer acquisition (CAC)

Case Study: How Thnx! Created A Revenue-Positive Marketing Campaign With 100 Percent Conversion Rates (Figure 2.6)

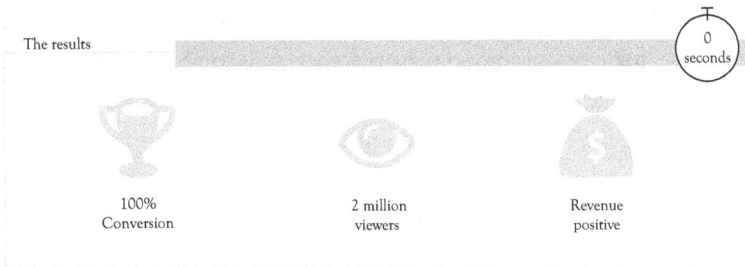

The results

| | | | 0 seconds |

100%
Conversion

2 million
viewers

Revenue
positive

Figure 2.6 Zero second case study results

The Challenge

Gratitude technology company Thnx! faced the typical challenge of being relatively unknown and having no significant budget with which to change that. The Thnx! app allowed you to send a token of your gratitude digitally, which the recipient was able to exchange for a real cup of coffee. Thnx! captured the perfect way to acknowledge extra efforts by team members at work, without the typical awkwardness of a bunch of flowers or the jealousy associated with more significant gestures such as bonuses. The startup knew that to get scale, they would need an approach that did not rely on AdWords.

Fortunately, the team recognized that their association with gratitude was both timely and newsworthy. As one of their early investors noted, "You would have to be an ass to say no to gratitude." Thnx! leveraged this to create two remarkable launch activations that generated revenue and had perfect conversion rates.

The Approach

The team leveraged research linking gratitude with increased staff performance and used that to create a corporate good news story. The strategies for launching Thnx! achieved site traffic at scale with no financial outlay, generated revenue, and achieved 100 percent conversion rates—unheard of results in most marketing departments.

The marketing strategy consisted of two parts:

1. Thnx! approached a local and well-known coffee brand with a pitch for cross-promotion: would they sponsor 5,000 free coffees in exchange for an association with "gratitude" and a slot on early morning TV? The opportunity gave the coffee brand an easy way to align with gratitude and drive traffic to their stores. For the TV network, the segment provided fresh and interesting coverage with no effort on their part. Win–win–win. Thnx! had over 5,000 downloads in the two days after the piece was aired on morning TV.
2. The launch caught the attention of Microsoft, who, as it turned out, had a vested interest to deliver a token of gratitude to their loyal partner network to smooth over a few bumps from the previous year. Microsoft used our technology to open their annual conference in Last Vegas to a live audience of 35,000 people, with a further 2 million watching the live stream. In the opening 3 minutes, Gavriella Schuster, the former VP of Partnerships at Microsoft, sent 10,000 Thnx! to partners in the audience. The coffees were all redeemed within 72 hours.

Why It Worked

The strategies which drove thousands of Thnx! app downloads and delivered 100 percent conversion rates worked because:

1. The team had extreme clarity around what they needed to do to "make life better" for the launch partners. The TV needed fresh and exciting content; the coffee brand needed an interesting and socially responsible marketing hook; Microsoft needed a gesture of positivity to turn their partner vibe back to positive.

2. The limited coffee giveaways activated both the scarcity and free decision shortcuts.

3. Instead of promoting their app on their own, Thnx! leaned on the advocacy of others activating the credibility decision shortcut.

4. The combination of activating social proof, credibility, and the power of free, coupled with the low resistance of deep linking to preload coffee vouchers into the Thnx! app significantly shortened the buying process, effectively removing all obstacles and making the decision to download Thnx! an easy choice.

Apply It in Your Business

We found that the companies with best-in-class partnership programs generate a greater share of their revenue from the partnership chan-nel, drive faster revenue growth within the channel and at the overall company level, and are more likely to exceed stakeholder expectations on business metrics than companies with less mature partnership programs.

—Forrester Research, 2021

To drive traffic to your website using a strategy other than Google AdWords, look for opportunities to:

1. Reach your target audience at scale. Instead of marketing in sin-gle units, are there ways to get in front of potential buyers at scale through associations, adjacent businesses, and businesses that aggre-gate your target audience?

2. Establish a partnership with a node by solving their problems. For example, associations often need to remain relevant to their members, banks need to align with social good initiatives, and mining companies with renewables. Solve for their needs—make their life better.

3. Create an offer that will activate a number of the decision shortcuts described in Part I. A powerful combo is a one-click activation that is limited, promoted by a credible partner node, and offers a discount or free sample.

Summary

The Zero Seconds ADORE milestone is the moment that a new site visitor lands on your website. It is the point of arrival, or the inception point of the relationship between the new site visitor and your brand. The chapter considered the mechanics and economics of search engine optimization (SEO) and explored alternate strategies to drive traffic to your website.

Ten Seconds

The First Impression

Introduction: Does It Feel Right?

This chapter will show you how to:

1. Reduce high bounce rates
2. Improve your average time on site

The first Ten Seconds milestone starts the moment your site visitor lands on your website. The Zero Second milestone looked at the strategies for getting the site visitor to your website. In the Ten Seconds milestone, we look at what happens immediately after the site visitor arrives (Figure 2.7).

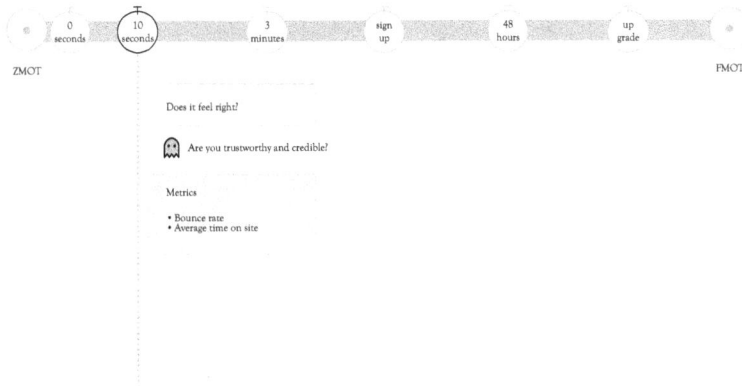

Figure 2.7 The Ten Second milestone of the ADORE process™

Our subconscious mind processes, first impressions between humans in a matter of milliseconds (Ludden 2017). If you were to view that moment in slow motion, you would see a vast range of inputs such as height, stature, clothing, appearance, smell, posture, gait, being filtered by our past experiences, prejudices, and biological preferences steeped in our very DNA. In a digital context, the process is much the same, although the time frame is a fraction slower and the inputs are the digital equivalent of personal attributes.

In a digital context, you typically have less than ten seconds to form the right first impression. In this time, your site visitor will be processing input variables to ascertain whether or not your website feels right—and make the critical decision of whether you will receive any more of their attention. If the answer is yes, you will have succeeded in guiding your site visitor through the Ten Second milestone, and they will be ready to go on to their next level of commitment, the Three Minute milestone.

Your Ten Second milestone, or digital first impression, is made up of two critical elements:

1. Vibe and visuals, and
2. Value Proposition

Vibe and Visuals

The digital equivalent of "looking good" is made up of lots of small elements that together create your visual first impression. The colors, fonts, imagery, language, and general composition of the hero part of your home (or landing) page collectively create a sense, or vibe, that is ingested by your site visitor. These factors work together to establish a first impression of trust—does your brand feel right? Do I trust you? Observe your own behavior as you navigate websites over the next week and pause each time you bounce off a prospective brand's site. What was it that made you leave? Did you on some level question the credibility of the brand? (Figure 2.8)

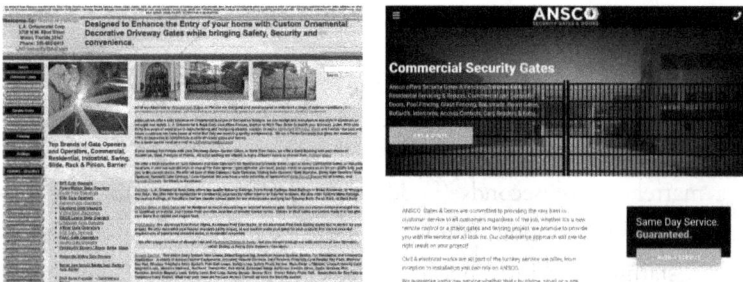

Figure 2.8 How vibe and visuals contribute to trustworthiness and credibility

Value Proposition

In addition to the visual vibe, your value proposition, or the words in the hero part of your website, are an essential element in forming the first impression. Your value proposition gives a shortcut answer for attention-poor consumers to the question of "How do you make my life better?" It is your chance to make an instant case for why it is that this site visitor should spend more than Ten Seconds on your website.

Once again, once you start looking, you'll get a sense of the types of value propositions you are responsive to. For example, Slack "makes it downright pleasant to work together," Airtasker "connects you with experts to get the job done," Thinkific "powers your education empire." In less than Ten Seconds and around ten words, great brands let you know how it is that they can make your life better. Your website needs to do the same.

Anxieties at Ten Seconds

To pass through the Ten Second milestone, your site visitor needs to have their preloaded anxieties alleviated. When you meet a human, the "I don't know what it was, it just felt wrong" flags waved by your intuition give you warning signs that may not yet correspond to input variables. In the digital parallel, the anxieties or gut instincts that come up for your site visitors at this stage are "are you trustworthy and credible?"

It is common to see brands add credibility and trust to their value proposition by leaning on common decision shortcuts (refer to Part I). This is typically captured in impressive statistics displayed very close to the value proposition. Imagine that you are considering rebuilding your website and land on the WordPress site. Within the first Ten Seconds, your fears are allayed when you discover that "WordPress is the world's most popular website, 41 percent of the Internet is built on WordPress." The reference to social proof and credibility decision shortcuts trigger our natural impulses to be persuaded, effectively removing anxieties and seamlessly propelling us to the Three Minute milestone.

Common Causes of Issues

Indications that you have issues at the Ten Second milestone typically present as high bounce rates or very low average time on site.

A note that, as with all metrics, it's important to understand what each metric means in your marketing analysis tool or dashboard, and to be aware that each tool may have slight variations in how the metrics are computed. As an example, Google calculates bounce rates as requests to the server. So technically, if you have a simple, static HTML page that loads completely with only one request to the server and no other pages on your website, Google could report all your sessions as "bounced." The practical likelihood that your website falls into this edge case is close to nil, so in general, if your website is reporting bounce rates of 80 percent or higher, it is worth investigating.

Another way to spot issues at the Ten Second milestone is to monitor the average time on your site. If your metrics are really low, in the range of under one minute, then it is likely that you can improve the Ten Second milestone of your website, which will lead to more site visitors being in the running for forming a relationship with your brand.

The most typical causes of issues at Ten Second milestone are:

1. Failure to establish trust through your visuals and vibe
2. Unclear or internally focused value proposition

Visuals and Vibe Fail to Establish Trust

The first cause of issues, failure to establish trust through visuals and vibe, can be resolved by making changes to your brand style or investing in the conscious development of a brand style guide. A good style guide will create the right input variables to promote trust and alleviate any anxieties that arise when a first impression is made.

It may be tempting to overlook the importance of developing a solid style guide, and I often see this with brands that have been in market for a long time and typically rely on handshakes to close B2B deals. However, the reality is that the landscape has changed. If your brand is not well known, for example, if you are expanding into a new market, the absence of a great first impression may preclude your chances of making it onto the shortlist of brands under consideration.

Value Proposition Is Unclear

The second cause of issues, an unclear or inward-focused value proposition, is one of the most commonly occurring problems for brands expanding into new markets. In new markets, nobody knows you, so you have to work a little harder to tell them why you are worth engaging with.

A value proposition is "the promise of value to be delivered" to your future customer. Most brands trip up because they use the value proposition to communicate why they get out of bed in the morning instead of focusing on how they make life better for their customer.

Value is measured in the currency of your audience.

One of the critical things to remember when adjusting your value proposition is that value is measured in the currency of your audience. You may have an ambitious goal of "making life better for all citizens," but as a value proposition, those words tell me little of how you will make my life better. Lack of clarity puts the onus on your site visitor to figure it out—will you make my life better through shoes, or software, or organic juices? Giving your site visitor homework is a tremendous blocker, not only at the Three Minute milestone but at every milestone.

How to Fix Issues

Fixing issues at the Ten Second milestone will reduce your bounce rates and open the door to engagement with your brand. There are two main ways to do this.

Develop a Brand Style Guide

A style guide is a system of using elements of visual communication to represent your brand (Figure 2.9). It is what forms the first impression of your brand in a digital space and is much like your first impression in person. Just as you would iron a shirt before going to a job interview, paying attention to how you use color, font, images, and language will instantly add credibility and trust to your digital presence.

Note that your style guide need not win any awards. In most cases, it is enough to simply develop a consistent and clear way of communicating with your target audience. Paying attention to things like the use of color and introducing visual hierarchy to your primary and secondary call to action (CTA) links and buttons will get you significant payoffs.

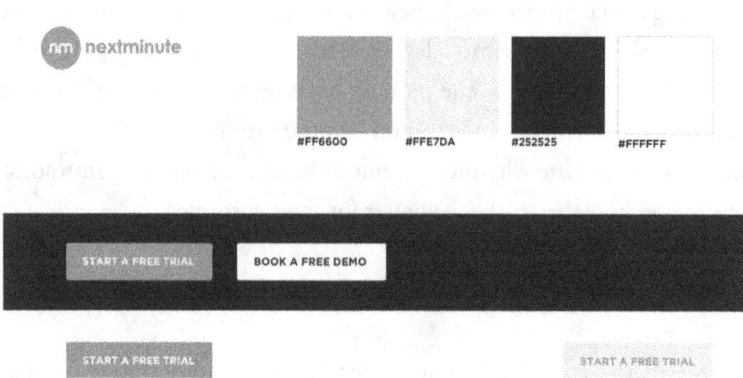

Figure 2.9 A simple style guide showing the color palette for NextMinute and the use of color to depict primary and secondary CTAs

Develop a Clear Value Proposition

Crafting a clear value proposition is not easy. Although the result is only a few words, coming up with the right few words is an art form that is often easier to tackle with the help of an outside contributor or copywriter. If you are tackling this on your own, lean on the worksheets at the end of this chapter to get started.

To get your site visitor to walk through the Ten Second milestone, your challenge is to present your value in the best possible light. Make it easy for your site visitor to choose you by expressing this value in their currency. Be very clear about how your offering makes their life better.

How to Measure Success

The following metrics can measure success at the Ten Second milestone:

1. Bounce rates
2. Average time on site

Case Study: How a Decade of Brand Evolution Helped GoDaddy Appeal to a Larger Target Audience and Grow Online Sales (Figure 2.10)

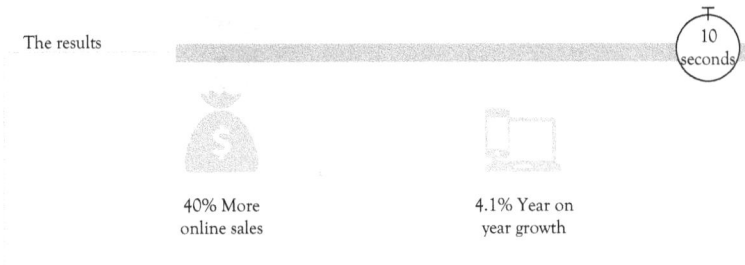

The results

10 seconds

40% More
online sales

4.1% Year on
year growth

Figure 2.10 Ten Second case study results

The Challenge

Founded in 1997, GoDaddy spent the first decade as the infamous, cringe-worthy brand associated with risqué marketing tactics featuring a trademarked GoDaddy Girl. Perhaps a brilliant strategy for early growth, the approach nevertheless alienated a large part of the potential target audience and certainly posed a blocker to customer loyalty. In a 2011 *Harvard Business Review* case study, the authors describe the tenuous nature of GoDaddy's brand love, as evidenced by a mass exodus of 72,000 customers in the course of one month. Although popular, the brand was tolerated rather than loved.

The Approach

The customer revolt in 2011 happened around the same time as a private equity injection of capital into the business. With that, came the expected mandate to scale and grow—and thus began a decade long evolution of the vibe, visuals, and value proposition of the brand (Figure 2.11).

Figure 2.11 A decade of GoDaddy brand identity and value proposition evolution

In 2010, the value proposition of GoDaddy was focused on their core business, "Domains for $1.99," endorsed by a jacket clad GoDaddy Girl. The brand's logo looked visually unchanged since 2001: the "quirky" (some say creepy) dude with green glasses continued to promise "hot" prices. The visuals start to change gradually in the next year, with 2012 seeing a transition in messaging to "searching for a domain," departing from the focus on "hot" pricing and cheap domains. While the GoDaddy Girl is now also customer, and the words take a step away from "hotness," we continue to witness ever plunging necklines and raunchy Super Bowl ads featuring the GoDaddy Girl. The mixed messaging confuses the public, with the general opinion of the brand reported as "*Eyyyyyyeh*," somewhere between indifference and distaste.

A new CEO enters the scene, and with that, leads the brand to a new maturity. By 2013, the messaging changes significantly: GoDaddy is now the place to "Easily create a professional website." GoDaddy Girl is retired and replaced by very ordinary and relatable small business blokes, Roland Payne and E. Z. Smith.

GoDaddy went public by issuing an initial public offer (IPO) in 2015. By 2017, the brand has become almost generic in terms of the visual identity but remains focused in their messaging "Build a better website in under an hour." The creepy mascot is dropped from the logo around 2018, and the business is now squarely focused on appealing to a much larger small business market.

In 2020, GoDaddy relaunches their logo—loved by some, criticized by others as being a close copy to that of AirBnB. While differences of opinion abound regarding the design aesthetic, the brand successfully completes the transition from tasteless and alienating, to professional and helpful. GoDaddy becomes a brand that is loved by over 19.3 million customers around the globe, reflecting 11.5 percent revenue growth between 2019 and 2020, and a 40 percent increase in e-commerce sales.

Why It Worked

The evolution of the GoDaddy brand image and message worked for several reasons:

1. Over a period of 10 years, the updated visuals changed the vibe of the first impression from tacky to trustworthy, creating an increasing sense of credibility through updated fonts, colors, messaging, and use of imagery.
2. The shift away from using "sex" to sell, to speaking to ways in which GoDaddy could make life better for customers dramatically improved the ability for the brand to be related to, and loved, by a larger target audience.
3. The updated visuals made it easier for site visitors to get to know GoDaddy. While cheap tricks and clickbait headlines do drive traffic, the traffic is often shallow and does not lead to meaningful engagement. Featuring relatable small business owners and an updated brand image opens the door to discovery and removes resistance from the first impression (Figure 2.12).

Apply It in Your Business

If your brand is losing business to competing firms, and you notice that the time on site for your website is relatively low, you can improve your chances of success by investing in your Ten Second milestone in three easy ways:

1. Check that your brand looks visually credible. If your styling is outdated, invest in a brand refresh.
2. Check that your value proposition is clear. If it is not super obvious how you will make your site visitor's life better, there is worthwhile work to be done.

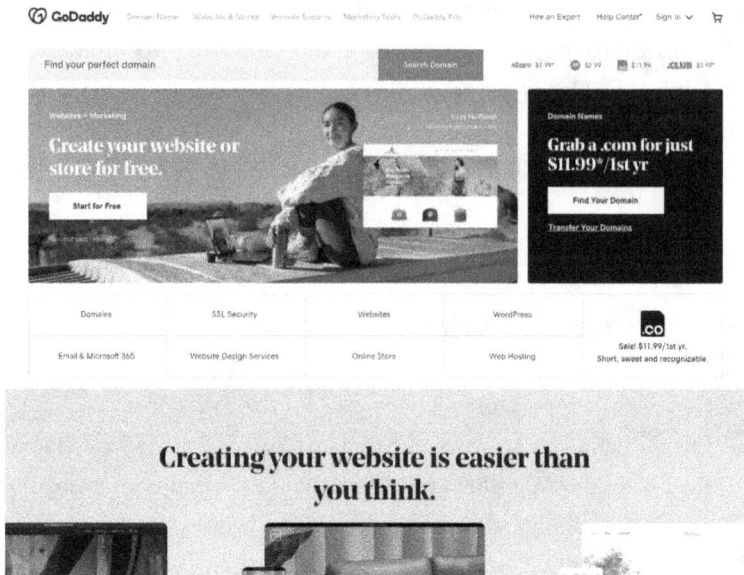

Figure 2.12 *The modernized elements lend credibility and open the door to engagement for new site visitors*

3. Check that your page headline (or value proposition) matches the copy on the referring website or ad. For example, suppose your site visitor clicked on a link for "setting up an e-commerce store" and landed on a page about "cheap domain names." The disconnect introduced by different copy may disorient your site visitor and cause them to leave.

Summary

The Ten Second ADORE milestone is the first impression that your website creates for a new site visitor. In these first few seconds, your newly landed site visitor will do a subconscious assessment of a multitude of variables, including colors, fonts, branding, general aesthetic, value proposition, and the overall vibe to determine whether your website "feels right." Failing to capture a site visitor's attention at this stage reduces your chances of converting the site visitor into a customer to almost zero, rendering this portion of your marketing budget totally ineffective. High bounce rates and low average times on site are good indicators that your Ten Second milestone may need some work.

Three Minutes

The First Date

Introduction: Why Should I Stay?

This chapter will show you how to:

1. Improve your average time on site
2. Improve your average number of page visits
3. Improve your average number of return visitors

If you have successfully got your site visitor to your website and managed to establish a credible first impression, well done! Your next mission is to get the site visitor to succeed at the Three Minute milestone. The Three Minute moment is your digital first date—it is your opportunity to reveal the key elements of your brand and convince the site visitor that it is worth their while to get to know your brand at a deeper level (Figure 2.13).

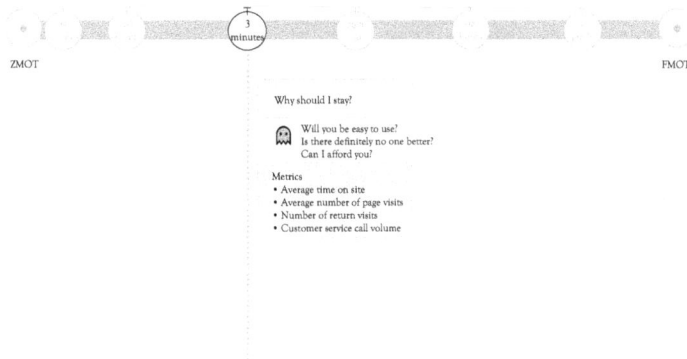

3 minutes

ZMOT

FMOT

Why should I stay?

Will you be easy to use?
Is there definitely no one better?
Can I afford you?

Metrics
- Average time on site
- Average number of page visits
- Number of return visits
- Customer service call volume

Figure 2.13 The Three Minute milestone of the ADORE process™

Three Minutes May Take Longer and May Take
Multiple Return Visits

Note that the three-minute timeframe for this milestone assumes a typical B2C e-commerce scenario. The three minutes of engagement with your website may consist of multiple return visits to your website. Your prospective buyer may look you up while waiting for a dental appointment, be interrupted, and pick up the thread a few days later over a glass of wine after dinner. In some cases, such as technical B2B purchases, the three minutes may take months.

The important thing about the Three Minute milestone is that it is the moment at which your site visitor is ready to take the next step and form an active commitment with your brand. Recall from the consistency and scarcity decision shortcuts that the moment a site visitor takes an active role in their exploration of your brand, you will be triggering in them a sense of ownership. When this happens, they become drawn toward completing the process to maintain their sense of consistency. Thus, if you can get the site visitor through the Three Minute milestone, you make the next step of active participation almost inevitable.

Anxieties at Three Minutes

As with all of the ADORE milestones, in order for your site visitor to continue on their journey past the Three Minute milestone, they will have to have all anxieties and fears alleviated. Reflect for a moment on times where you have stopped short of filling out a form to download a whitepaper or abandoned the sign-up process for a demo or product trial. If you think back to these moments, it is likely that your decision to discontinue your journey with that brand was due to one of these reasons:

1. The resistance to sign-up was too high.
2. You questioned whether the offering would be easy to use.
3. You questioned whether there was definitely no one better.
4. You questioned whether you could afford it.

Once again, what makes the ADORE process™ so universal is that these anxieties come up for buyers at this stage regardless of what type of thing is being bought. These anxieties are as true for buyers of electric vehicles as they are for buyers of enterprise sales automation software.

Common Causes of Issues

There is a good chance that you may have inefficiencies or issues at the Three Minute milestone if you have:

1. Low average time on site
2. Low average number of page views
3. Low return visitors
4. High volume of customer enquiries of the "How do I find..." nature

Recall that the ADORE Three Minute milestone will likely consist of multiple return visits to your website, so these three metrics (average time, average page views, and return visitors) need to be interpreted together. As a guide, if your site visitors are spending more than three minutes on your site, you have acceptable return visit rates (40%+), and if people can find what they need, then you're going well. If not, then there is work to be done.

How to Fix Issues

The most common cause of issues at the ADORE Three Minute milestone is the failure of your website to take the site visitor on a journey of escalating commitment—in other words, you are not telling your brand story in the correct order. For example, imagine that a prospective buyer lands on your landing page and the only instruction for them is to "Buy Now." While some customers may be immediately ready to take that action, the ones who are arriving at your website for the first time may not be ready yet. Giving them an option to "Learn More" or "Request Demo" invites them in and allows them to feel like they are in control of how fast the relationship with your brand is progressing (Figure 2.14).

Unfold Your Brand Story in the Right Order

To fix issues at the Three Minute milestone, start with the brand story you completed in the previous chapter and add to it the buying process

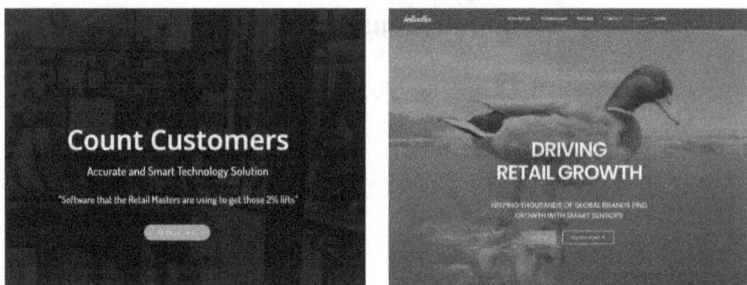

Figure 2.14 The elements on your page direct the site viewer toward an action: On the left, a new site visitor is invited to talk; on the right, a new site visitor is invited to buy or request a demo if they are not ready

of your highest value customers. The worksheets in this chapter will guide you through that. Once you have the elements, you need to place them on your home page (or landing page) in an order that sequentially deepens the relationship with your future buyer. Recall that the formula for love developed at the State University of New York hinged on the sequence in which the questions were asked. In the same way, your challenge is to unfold your brand story in the right order so that you create increasing commitment while alleviating any fears that crop up.

The specific order of elements on the home page, shown below and included as a worksheet at the end of this chapter, was derived from a 2016 study of 100 open-source product websites that sold a premium version of their product. At the time, I was interested in how the most successful open-source companies managed to overcome the considerable challenge of competing against their own free products. The analysis revealed that the home pages were all structured in a similar way, which happened to align with the patterns of escalating commitment in the formula for love. Of course, correlation does not imply causation on its own—however, having tested this home page template in hundreds of scenarios, with dozens of different target audiences, with 100 percent success rates, will give you confidence that this is a great starting point for your own website.

Know when to break the rules (Figure 2.15).

The $39 billion acquisition of Afterpay by Square tells a perfect 10-year, overnight success story. From a digital footprint perspective, it is also a perfect example of understanding the rules of engagement, and having confidence to break them at the right time.

| 2018 | 2019 | 2021 |

Figure 2.15 *Understand the rules and know when to break them. Afterpay's home page demonstrates the transition from a "typical" home page layout, to one that breaks the rules to great effect*

Afterpay was founded in 2014, and for the first five years, it focused its brand messaging and brand story on the mechanics of the Afterpay platform. Four easy payments, instant gratification. The brand story explained the why and the how. Notably, this was a new product in market, and there was an element of education that had to take place before the brand itself became a verb.

In 2019, Afterpay starts to break the rules in terms of their home page, shifting from a focus on what and how, to a focus on how they make life better for the consumer. Today, the home page looks more like a digital shopping mall rather than a consumer credit facility.

The Optimal Home Page Layout

To fix issues at the Three Minute milestone and get your site visitors to step into the next level of commitment with your brand, review your home page to ensure that its elements are presented in the following order.

Hero Section

The hero section of your website communicates your Ten Second first impression. It is typically made up of:

1. Value proposition. Articulate precisely how you make their life better.
2. Evidence of best. Add instant credibility through research endorsements and social proof.

3. Primary CTA. Provide a fast track to the action that you most desire the site visitor to take, assuming that they are already familiar with your brand.

4. Secondary CTA. Provide a "welcome and learn more" fast track for those who are not yet ready to commit (Figure 2.16).

Figure 2.16 Salesforce and Tradify hero sections showing a clear value proposition, credibility, and a clear CTA

The configuration of these elements in the Hero section, coupled with the right visual aesthetic for your brand, activates three powerful decision shortcuts in your site visitors: social proof, credibility, and the power of free. These activate a powerful habitual response and lay the foundation for the consistency decision shortcut that we will activate in the Sign-up and Upgrade milestones.

Featured Premium Products (Optional)

You can use banners or special promotional features and elements to activate the decision shortcut for scarcity in your site visitors. This is particularly powerful to draw attention to something new that you are offering, draw attention to items you get a good margin on, or move items more quickly (Figure 2.17).

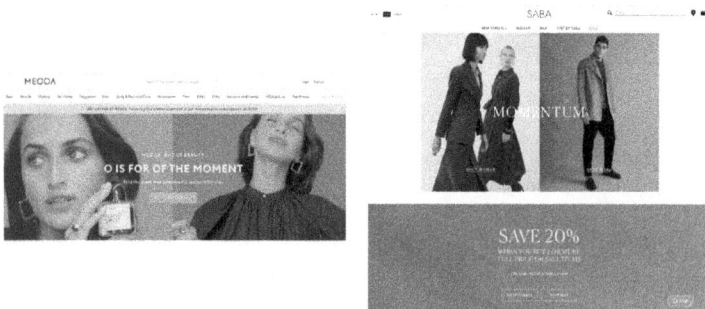

Figure 2.17 Examples of banners promoting featured items at MECCA and Saba

User Stories and Social Proof

At this point, you have told your site visitor how you make their life better and leaned on credibility through association with authority or an impressive fact (like we are used by 500 million people every day). Before you launch into details about why and how, use the power of social proof and the advocacy of others to promote your brand for you—recall that, according to Harvard Research, other people's advocacy is the most powerful impetus to buy.

The use of social proof and user stories (Figure 2.18) at the top of your home page also sends a clear message that your site visitor is not alone—that other people just like them (whether actually or aspirationally) use products like yours.

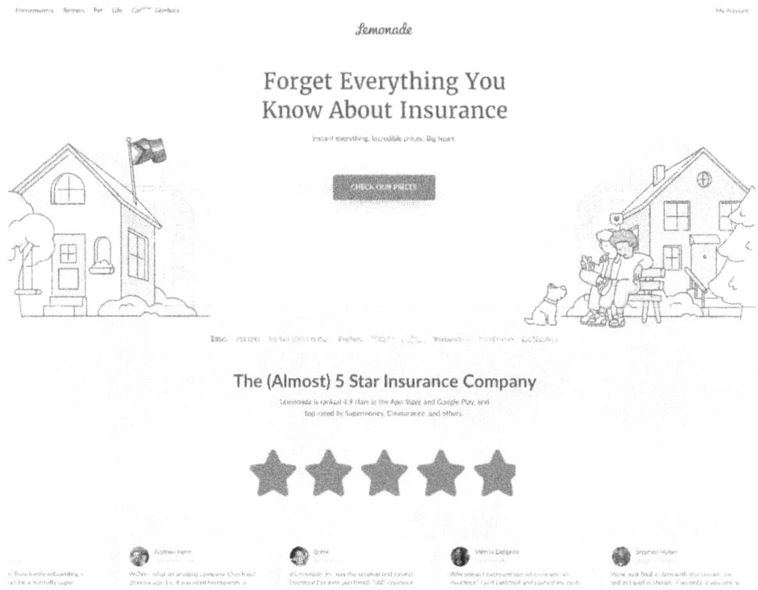

Figure 2.18 User stories and social proof give comfort and a sense that you are not alone

What You Are Offering

It's time to unfold the first layer of detail about what your offer actually is. Leaving this any longer may leave the site visitor disinterested, as the overhead of figuring out what it is, if left much longer, would be too high.

Take care to express your what in clear, concise language from the customer's perspective (Figure 2.19). As a rule of thumb, if you are describing your internal business processes, you are likely not expressing things from your customers' perspective.

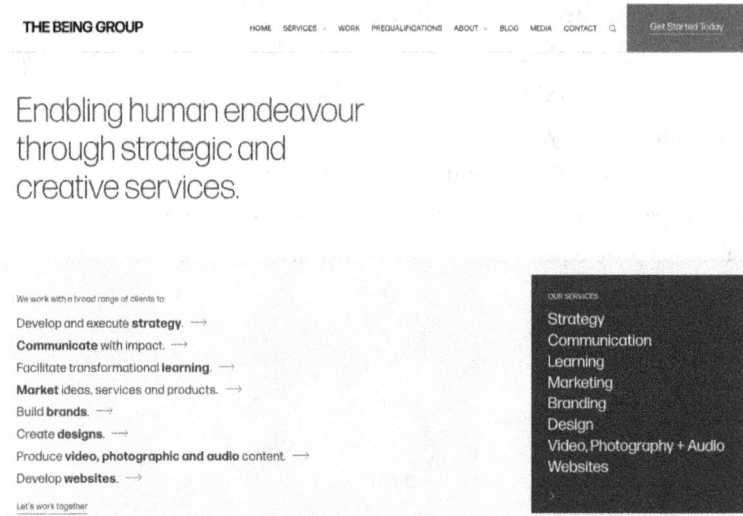

Figure 2.19 Clear articulation of what is on offer at the Being Group

This section also lays a soft foundation that will justify your pricing model by activating the anchoring and consistency decision shortcuts.

What to Expect

Clarity around the model of engaging with your brand is critical to alleviating fears that your potential buyers will have around "will you be easy to work with" (Figure 2.20). It also sets the baseline for expectations, which, as you will recall, is the point from which satisfaction is measured.

Demonstrate Trustworthiness

This element needs to communicate that you have their back, you can be trusted, and you will be there for them. For technical products, you could reference patents, ISO certification, or similar; for consumer goods, it could be hassle-free returns (Figure 2.21).

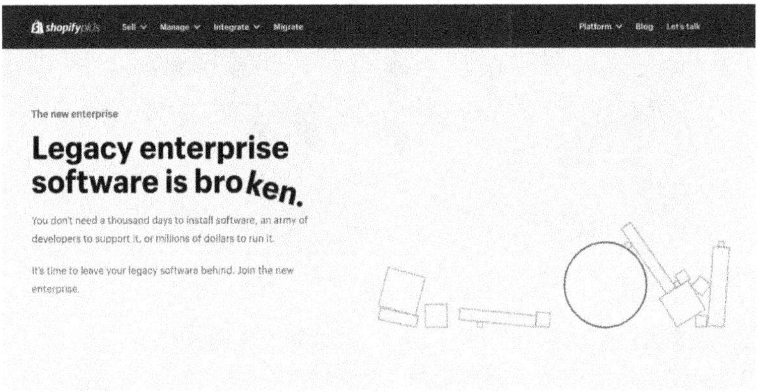

Figure 2.20 Shopify Plus anticipates anxieties and resistance and addresses them directly

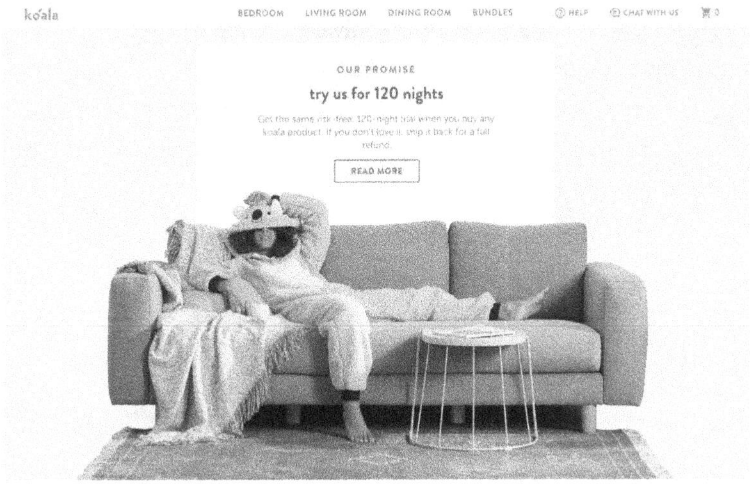

Figure 2.21 Koala's success was powered by their risk-reducing four-month no-questions returns policy

Hints of How

The home page is not the place to tell your site visitor everything (Figure 2.22). You simply need to flag that you have the answers, should they have more questions. You can include links to blog posts or white papers; however, resist the temptation to tell your new site visitor too much. The relationship needs to evolve at the right pace—you don't want to tell them absolutely everything on the first date.

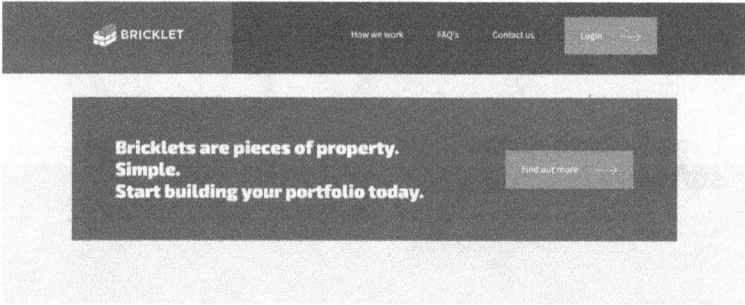

Figure 2.22 Bricklet offers a new fragmented ownership model for property—you get a hint on the home page, with an invitation to learn more

Testimonials for a Strong Finish

The final section of your page is the equivalent of the window display that you see on the way out of the shop—it is there to close the deal. Finish your home page with strong testimonials or further social proof to eliminate any lingering doubts (Figure 2.23). Ideally, if you have insights into the main reasons why people do not buy from you, finish on a testimonial that addresses these directly.

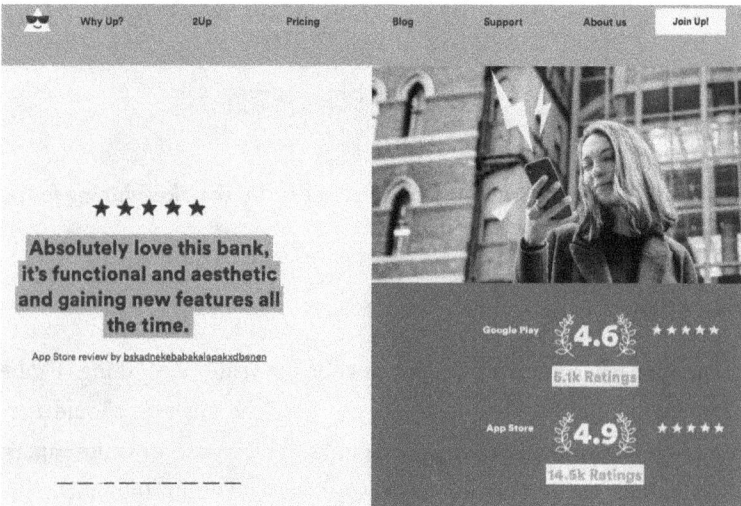

Figure 2.23 Up Bank's fresh and unexpected design is backed by powerful testimonials and social proof

The optimal home page template is a solid place to start from, and like everything in life that verges on the sublime, once you have mastered the basics, you can, for good reason, introduce deviations or adaptations (Figure 2.24). Doing this with an understanding of the impacts that it will have on your buyers' evolving relationship with your brand is vital. For example, you may adapt the home page template to a promotional landing page by shifting the focus to scarcity and reducing the call to actions to fast-track the journey toward commitment.

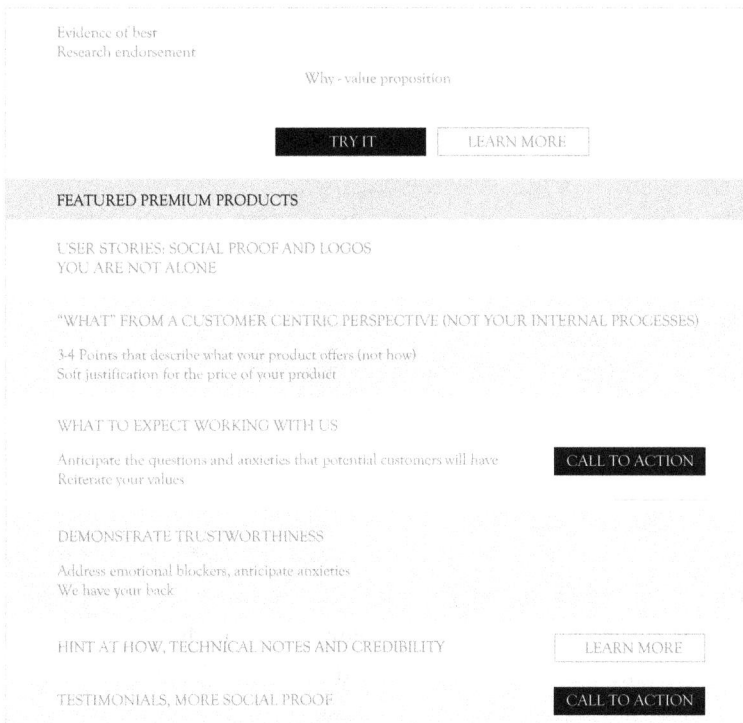

Figure 2.24 How to order elements on the home page for optimal performance

How to Measure Success

The following metrics can measure success at the Three Minute milestone:

1. Average time on site
2. Average number of page visits

3. Number of return visits

4. Volume of customer service enquiries about finding the right information. Pro-tip here: capture frequently occurring questions and fold them into your website at the logical point where the questions arise.

Case Study: How NextMinute Reduced Website Exits by 170 Percent by Creating a Smoother Journey to Sign-Up (Figure 2.25)

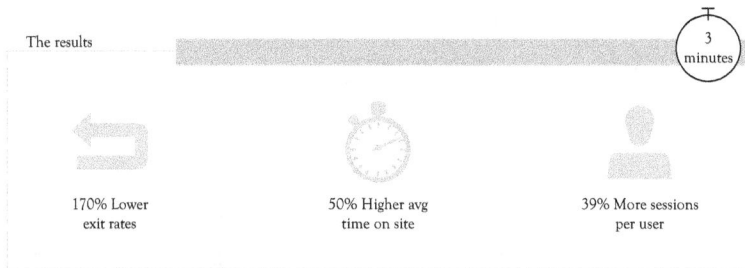

Figure 2.25 Three Minute case study results

The Challenge

NextMinute is a SaaS job management product suite for mid-sized construction firms such as builders, plumbers, electricians, and tilers. NextMinute was growing rapidly and looking to refine their go to market strategy in Australia. The sales team had excellent sales conversion rates from the demo session—the challenge facing the team was how to convince more site visitors to sign up for these sessions. The sales team also noted that they spent a lot of time explaining the offering and pricing model to prospective clients.

The Approach

An analysis of the NextMinute website revealed four areas for improvement:

1. Refining the value proposition
2. Refining the brand style guide

3. Refining the order in which information was presented on each page, and

4. Simplifying the pricing model

The original webpage hero led with the value proposition "Job management software designed by tradies (contractors) for tradies" and had three equally weighted CTA buttons in the top navigation bar (Figure 2.26). There were no further CTAs below the value proposition. Unfortunately, the equal weighting on the three CTAs provided no guidance as to which action the site visitor should take—the need to make a decision introduced a tiny but real moment of resistance.

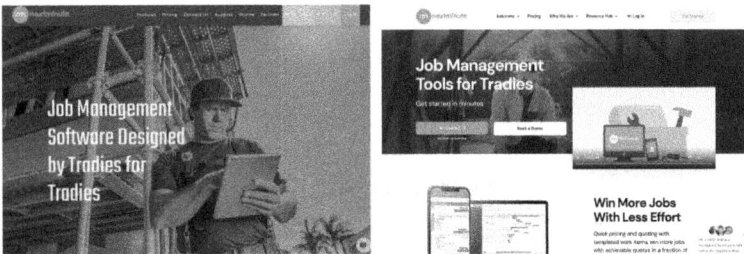

Figure 2.26 Before and after designs of the home page hero

The hero section layout and copy were changed to reflect the main reason why high-value customers were using the brand, that being ease of use. Loyal brand advocates often spoke of how much easier NextMinute was to use and engage with than larger competitors. The new hero section copy was updated to "Job management tools for Tradies. Get started in minutes." This was coupled with a primary CTA to "Get started," with an anxiety-reducing "No credit card needed" below the button. A secondary CTA to book a demo was introduced. The buttons in the top navigation bar were removed, leaving only a single CTA to "Get Started." Introducing a clear visual hierarchy in these CTAs removed the resistance of having to stop and make a decision.

The brand style guide was updated to include the visual hierarchy for CTA buttons on the site. A modern color palette and font selection were chosen. The original imagery was retained as it showed real and relatable images of NextMinute's customers using the product in the field.

The information presented on the home and landing pages was reordered in line with the recommendations in the home page templates (which you can download at the end of this chapter) (Figure 2.27). The pricing model was also simplified—removing the "calculator" and introducing two clear, explained options that delineated between "admin users" (bookkeepers or business owners) and "mobile users" (contractors working on jobs).

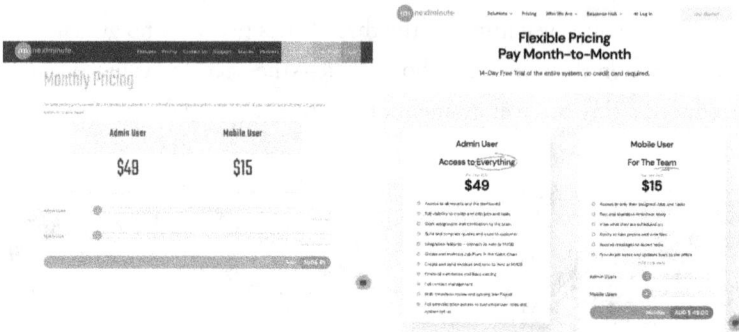

Figure 2.27 The old pricing page created confusion as site visitors could not immediately understand what Admin and Mobile users were. The updated page made the distinction clear, removing blockers and increasing demo booking rates

Why It Worked

The changes made to the NextMinute website are an excellent example of how the six ADORE steps can be used together to create stronger brand buyer relationships. Identifying the four main areas that were below optimal levels (value proposition, styling, page layouts, and pricing model) allowed the team to make relatively simple changes to the website, which resulted in immediate and significant improvements to the performance of their prime digital asset.

> *Our website is now properly aligned with what our visitors are looking for and presented in a way that leads them down the right path of education and qualification. On top of this, ADORE has given us the framework to create and distribute new content that fits with this journey, which we can then use to generate more traffic through SEO and social distribution.*
>
> —Hayden Foster, CEO, NextMinute

The changes made worked for the following reasons:

1. The new value proposition provided a hook that resonated with the main reason customers loved NextMinute: ease of use. Removing the words "designed for tradies by tradies" sharpened the focus on what was important. Fewer words in the hero equal more impact, as they reduce the cognitive load in that first few seconds of orientation for a new site visitor. The change resulted in 170 percent lower exit rates from the website.

2. Introducing a visual hierarchy for the CTAs had the immediate effect of reducing cognitive load, and at the same time, directing the site visitor toward the desired action. The changes resulted in a 50 percent increase in average time on site, indicating that site visitors were more interested and engaged.

3. Changing the order in which information was displayed on the key pages improved the unfolding of the NextMinute brand story, resulting in site visitors becoming more engaged as they understood what the offer was and how it would make their life better. These changes resulted in a 39 percent increase in the number of sessions per user, and the average session per user increased by 200 percent. These repeat visits cumulatively increase the site visitor's commitment to NextMinute, activating the consistency decision shortcut.

4. The last change, simplifying the pricing model, reduced the cognitive load and burden previously placed on the site visitor in having to think hard to figure it out. The change was effective as it activated several core decision shortcuts, *free*, relative comparison, and the removal of obstacles. The change has increased the number of demo bookings and reduced the callers' confusion around the NextMinute model.

We are only seeing an exit rate of 27 percent compared to 47 percent on our website conversion page, meaning users are more informed to convert.

—Hayden Foster, CEO, NextMinute

Apply It in Your Business

If you are reviewing your marketing strategy and considering expanding your sales and marketing team with new hires, use the ADORE process™

to first analyze your existing digital footprint. You may still find that the new hires are justified, but in optimizing the flow of site visitors into more committed phases of your customer journey, you will be releasing your new hires to focus on closing deals rather than answering basic questions about how your offering works.

Look for the signs that your website may need a tune-up at the Three Minute milestone. If you notice low return visit rates and low time on site, it is a good indication that applying the strategies that NextMinute used will help to increase your conversion rates to the next milestone, Sign-up. In particular:

1. Review the order in which you reveal your brand's story, paying attention to the cadence at which you invite the site visitor into forming a relationship with your brand.
2. Remove friction by making it easier for your site visitor to choose the action you want them to take.
3. Review your value proposition and styling, as it will impact the previous two points due to the visual nature of interactions in the digital space.

Summary

The Three Minute ADORE milestone represents the engagement between your site visitor and the unfolding of your brand story. In a digital world, three minutes is a long time—and an indicator that the site visitor who landed on your website is interested in your brand. The "three minutes" may consist of multiple visits to your website, and depending on sector, may actually be longer than three minutes (for example, complex machinery or engineering services). The important metrics to track at this milestone are average time on site, average return visits, and average number of page views. These will give you an indication of whether you are effectively telling your brand story in an engaging way. The next step will be to ask the site visitor for a sign of their commitment by nudging them toward a Sign-up.

Sign-Up

The Honeymoon

Introduction: Should I Play With It?

This chapter will show you how to:

1. Improve your visitor to sign-up ratio
2. Improve your average user retention rates

Your buyer is standing at the Sign-up moment. To get to this point, you have done the expensive work of getting the traffic to your website (Zero Seconds), of passing the first impression test (Ten Seconds), and instilling a sense of credibility and trust in your future buyer (Three Minutes). If you succeed in getting your site visitor through the Sign-up milestone, you stand the very best chance of creating a loyal brand advocate. The implications of this are significant—Harvard research shows that loyalty generates 2.5 more revenue and that this revenue base is more resilient to economic downturns and recessionary conditions (Figure 2.28).

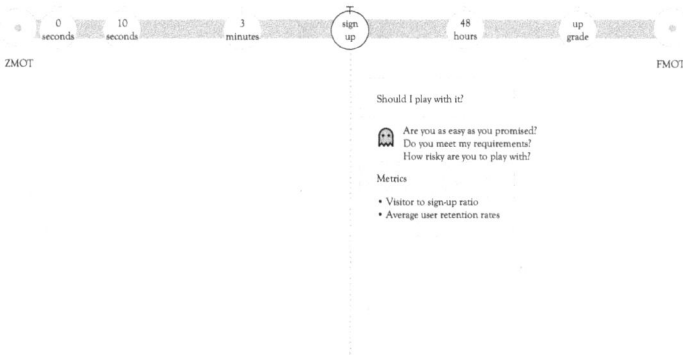

Figure 2.28 The Sign-up milestone of the ADORE process™

The Sign-up milestone represents the moment in the customer journey where your potential buyer makes a willing decision to enter into an exchange of value with your brand. The Sign-up moment may be a sign-up to a free trial, a sign-up to a demo, a newsletter, or registration for a webinar. The critical element is that this milestone involves an exchange of value—your potential buyer actively gives something up. The thing they give up is contextual and needs to be balanced off against resistance: for example, exchanging a work e-mail address for a useful report is generally acceptable, whereas most site visitors would resist providing a work e-mail address, and also a phone number, their role, their boss's name, and firstborn's age in exchange for the same report.

The process of giving something up triggers a number of powerful decision shortcuts, making it far easier for you to establish a connection and relationship with your future buyer. The decision shortcuts trigger a feeling of ownership, which, when coupled with the power of free, thrust the potential buyer into feeling a sense of loss before they complete the purchase. Your challenge is to create artifacts that will guide and incentivize your site visitor into making the Sign-up commitment while negating the powerful pull of the decision shortcut that pulls us to do nothing at all.

Duolingo, the language learning tool, does an excellent job of getting you committed to their product before even asking you to sign-up. Their onboarding process starts before you make an account. You get to play with the tool and fall in love with it—and only then do they nudge you toward sign-up. The process used by Duolingo removes all the resistance from the sign-up process.

Eliminate Resistance, but Hold Out on Full Value

The placement of the value exchange during the Sign-up milestone often takes a bit of finesse. The trick is to allow the site visitor to sample or play with your offering to the level that the next step of sign-up is inevitable. The tension is that it can be hard to balance removing all the resistance without giving up all the value for free. Influencer marketing company Scrunch faced this issue—they had many active users, with almost no conversion to the paid version of the product. Interviews with customers revealed that there was no incentive to sign-up, as they were able to get what they needed without creating an account. Simply placing a limit on the number of queries that could be run on Scrunch before triggering sign-up solved the issue.

Brands like Grammarly and Slack do this well. Grammarly gets you engaged and lets you spellcheck a certain number of documents before requiring you to sign up. They remove all the friction from getting started, give you a taste of the value that you can expect to receive, and when you are really getting into it, they nudge you to upgrade. Similarly, Slack lets you get set up and fully engaged with their product. They let you see the features you can't access and present you with an easy way to upgrade at the point you need to, such as when you want to invite someone from another team into your workspace. Keep an eye out for different techniques used by brands to place a wall between playing and paying for their product. TechCrunch is another example of this done well: to finish reading their most interesting articles, you are directed to sign up (Figure 2.29). Note that in this case they don't offer a free or trial period; the first part of the article is their sampler.

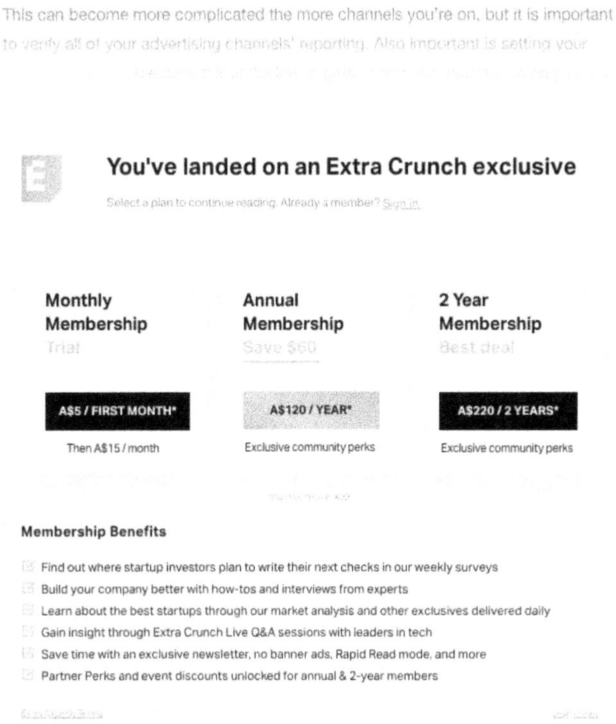

Figure 2.29 *TechCrunch lets you read partial articles before directing you to sign up*

Anxieties at Sign-Up

As your future buyer approaches the Sign-up milestone, they will be carrying a couple of residual anxieties:

1. Are you as easy as you promised?
2. Do you meet my requirements?
3. How risky are you to play with?

If you can successfully alleviate these fears, you're on your way to turning your site visitor into a loyal brand advocate.

Common Causes of Issues

Most typically, the causes of issues at the Sign-up gate involve an imbalance in the value exchange: asking the site visitor to give up too much in exchange for the value they perceive they will get after the exchange is complete. Indications that you can refine and improve the performance of your website at the Sign-up milestone include:

1. A low ratio of site visitors to sign-ups (or white paper downloads, or demo bookings)
2. A low rate of average user retention

If you are tracking metrics at a more detailed level, perhaps through tools like Hubspot, Pardot, or Hotjar, you may have more data points that you can investigate. In Part III, we'll look at how to effectively use data in the product design process. For now, take heart in the fact that while the detailed data can help you identify exact points of failure or confirm your intuition, the ratio of visitors to sign-ups is enough to know whether your brand relationship is optimized at this stage in the ADORE process™.

How to Fix Issues

There are a few common reasons that consistently decrease the performance of your website at the Sign-up milestone:

1. Too much friction to sign-up
2. Not enough need to sign-up
3. Perceived risk of signing up is too high
4. Pricing model is too complicated or unclear

Too Much Friction to Sign-Up

We have all experienced the effects of too much friction at the points of sign-up. When this happens, we simply abandon the process and return to the 34,999 other things we need to make decisions about that day. Form too long? Gone. Too many personal questions to sign up? Gone. Dodgy formatting or a redirect to a different looking site? Gone.

I often see businesses struggle with the Sign-up milestone when their offering is "complex" or "requires a lot of information to configure." If this applies to your business, you can significantly improve your sign-up rates if you reduce the overhead here and shift the collection of information into the onboarding experience. We'll look at this in detail in the next chapter, the First 48 Hours.

Not Enough Need to Sign-Up

The second common reason for low sign-up rates can be related to how your product is packaged. If the free version of your product serves the need or does the job well enough, there may simply be no impetus for the buyer to buy.

Typically, the fix here requires a reframing of what you charge for—remembering that value is perceived in the eye of your target audience and often does not correlate to the technical difficulty associated with the feature. One of my favorite examples here is the genius displayed by the Xbox team in charging young players $14 to change their username. This feature had zero technical cost (a database update) yet delivered infinite value to their young players. Xbox recognized that the username players choose at the age of six may no longer be on trend when they turn 13, and that the kids (would make outlandish promises to their parents) to have the ability to change their username rather than delete their account and lose their player status.

If your main competitor is your free product, consider repackaging your feature set to align with where your leading customers perceive value.

Perceived Risk of Signing Up Is Too High

The third reason why your sign-up rates may be low is that the perceived risk of signing up may be too high. Note that perceived risk has little to do with actual risk. It is simply the perception that your potential buyer has at the moment of sign-up.

In most cases, you can correct this by providing information earlier—recall from Part I that one of the only ways you can moderate expectations is by providing information. Every time you see the words "no credit card required," "cancel anytime," "you will not be charged until your trial runs out," or "free returns" placed before the buy now or sign-up moment, take note that these words are placed where they are solely to reduce your perceptions of risk. You know that this strategy works, and you know to what extent when you audit your monthly business or personal expenses every so often and find dozens of SaaS products that you forgot to cancel after the initial trial period.

Pricing Model Is Too Complicated or Unclear

The fourth main reason for suboptimal sign-up rates may be connected to your pricing model. If your pricing model requires three or four input variables, such as the number of people, the number of transactions, the number of locations, and the flavor of yogurt you had for breakfast, it's possible that your pricing model is creating an obstacle to signing up.

Another indicator that your pricing model is too complicated is if your sales team has trouble talking about your pricing structure to prospective customers. This is common in enterprise SaaS offerings but can also extend to industrial manufacturing or complex engineering-based solutions. The irony here is that pricing complexity often stems from a desire to be very fair, precise, and accurate. In most cases, the accuracy will be eschewed in favor of simplicity. Always remember that a human person makes the decision to sign up for your brand's offering in the context of their busy day. Simplifying your pricing page can have the effect of lifting your revenue and increasing your conversion rates.

Onside, a rural management SaaS offering, was struggling with explaining how they charged for different variants of their offering (Figure 2.30). The complexity stemmed from a desire to be fair. However, holding on to the idea of fairness blocked the team from recognizing that what they consider appropriate may not align with where the value lies in their target audience's eyes. The team deconstructed their offering and repackaged it by aligning the value points (i.e., real reasons why their customers were buying Onside) with their pricing bundles.

Figure 2.30 The pricing model on the left was complicated for site visitors to understand and the sales team to explain

The new pricing model has made it easier to communicate value to potential customers both digitally and also as part of the in-person sales process.

How to Measure Success

The following metrics can measure success at the Sign-up milestone:

1. Visitor to sign-up ratio
2. Average user retention rate

Case Study: Removing Resistance Results in 300 Percent More Sign-Ups for Compliance App Quipcheck (Figure 2.31)

The results

sign up

300% More sign-ups

Figure 2.31 Sign-up case study results

The Challenge

Quipcheck is a SaaS compliance check solution for plant and machinery. They provide a comprehensive checklist app that helps to reduce the administrative overheads in what is still essentially a paper-based industry. Quipcheck struggled with sub-5 percent sign-up rates, which they needed to rectify to grow their business into new markets. Their conversion rates after sign-up were great—the challenge was in getting site visitors to take the step to complete the "Get Started" process on their website.

The Approach

As you will recall from Part I, to get anyone to do anything, you need to remove the obstacles to make the desired behavior easy. Quipcheck changed their Sign-up form, removing a lot of the friction blocking more than 95 percent of potential buyers from filling the form (Figure 2.32). The simple change resulted in a 300 percent increase in demo bookings and inbound enquiries.

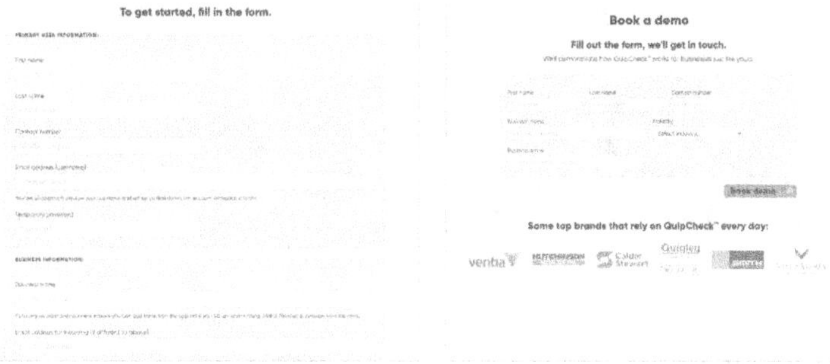

Figure 2.32 The Quipcheck form on the left asked the user to complete around 23 questions before sign-up. The updated form removed the obstacles and shifted the information collection to the new onboarding process in-app

Why It Worked

The approach worked as it removed the obstacles that were preventing site visitors from completing the sign-up process. Quipcheck had done a great job of getting their site visitors from Zero Seconds to the Sign-up milestone. Potential buyers were interested in starting the Sign-up process but gave up once they saw how many questions they had to fill out. The form was a real blocker.

The Quipcheck case is interesting, as the long sign-up form was introduced to help customize the app to the new user's needs. By removing the resistance from the sign-up form, the team needed to reimagine the onboarding process. The information required to customize the app was broken into smaller chunks and grouped into three easy onboarding steps. Note that while asking 20+ questions at sign-up was too much resistance, asking the same 20+ questions during a three-step onboarding process was totally fine (Figure 2.33). The results of this change were a significant increase in both sign-up rates and after sign-up retention rates.

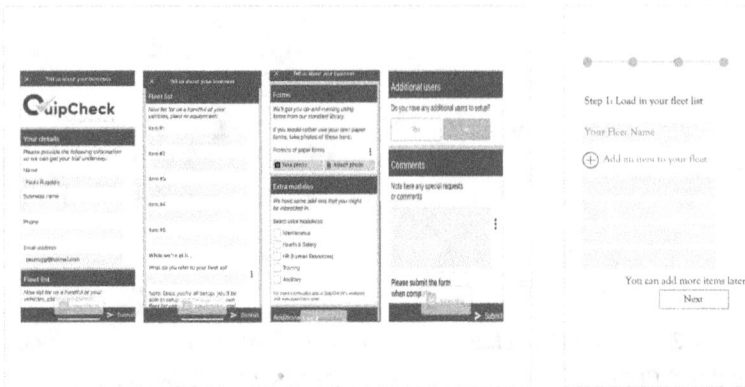

Figure 2.33 *Quipcheck chunked their onboarding information collection into a set of three simple steps, improving sign-up and retention rates*

The solution worked as initial resistance was removed. The information was requested in a serial way that matched the level of emotional commitment that the new customer was prepared to make to the brand.

Apply It in Your Business

Businesses that offer complex products often need extensive information to get a new user started in a meaningful way. You will be able to improve your sign-up and onboarding completion rates if you apply these two principles:

1. Remove as much resistance as possible from the sign-up process. In general, asking for contact info plus at most one other piece of information is the optimal tolerance level for new users.
2. Partition the information that you need to get the user started into logical groups to reduce the perceived cognitive load.
   (a) Ask for the information during onboarding, or
   (b) Start the user with sensible defaults and placeholder data.

Trello and LinkedIn are terrific examples of how information chunking and placeholder data containers guide new users without overwhelming them with too many instructions or questions. Quipcheck used these strategies to simplify their onboarding process and reduce the volume of top-level data in their in-app experience (Figure 2.34).

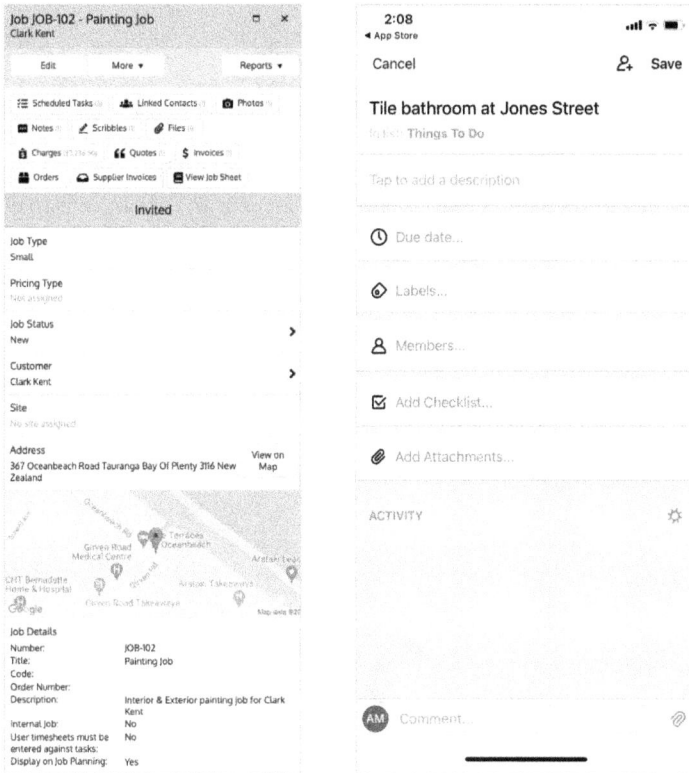

Figure 2.34 Quipcheck applied the strategies used by Trello to chuck information inside their app and reduce the overall amount of data at the highest level

Summary

The Sign-up ADORE milestone is a critical moment in the relationship arc between your site visitor and your brand, as it represents a moment of active commitment. When your site visitor Signs-up to a newsletter, free trial, or a gated piece of content, they are indicating that they are ready for the next phase in their relationship with your brand. Giving up an e-mail, a phone number, or investing time in considering a free trial are all strong indicators that your site visitor is engaged and interested. The important metric to track at this milestone is the ratio of site visitors to sign-ups. Once your potential customer has completed this milestone, you will need to shift focus to ensure that you can deliver a quick win or two in the moments right after Sign-up.

First 48 Hours

The Reality

Introduction: Can I Make It Work for Me?

This chapter will show you how to:

1. Improve your after sign-up churn rates.
2. Improve the effectiveness of your onboarding process.
3. Improve your engagement rates after sign-up.
4. Improve your task success rates.

What happens immediately after a customer signs on is one of the most overlooked moments in the customer journey. We typically put a lot of effort and expense toward attracting visitors to our website and then in getting them to the Sign-up milestone. And then we simply lose interest. We enter the digital equivalent of the disillusionment phase in human relationships, and like in human relationships, we turn our attention to attracting a new prospect, rather than focusing on the last mile in the relationship we just spent so much energy in cultivating.

Each time you lose a customer after sign-up, you steal from yourself.

We see examples of brands doing this all the time: banks would rather see loyal customers of 20 years walk away than spend any effort in reducing friction for the customers they have in hand. New technology start-ups pump millions into marketing efforts to attract new customers and give little attention to the churn rates at the back end of the process. In a recent study, Macquarie Bank reported that "buy now, pay later" platforms such as Afterpay have a huge loyalty problem. A study of 1,000 "buy now, pay later" users found that around 70 percent of respondents would not hesitate to change brands if their previous choice was not available. Despite fiercely low loyalty, Afterpay and others keep their marketing spend on full throttle and share prices buoyant by reporting only quarterly active customer numbers. The impact on their bottom line would be staggering if they shifted focus to reducing after sign-up churn and creating the conditions to foster lasting relationships with their users.

At the point that you have a signed-up customer, you have done all the hard persuasive work. The milestone of active commitment made when your site visitor signed up is an indication of unquestionable interest in your brand. The only thing you need to do now is deliver on the promises made by your brand during the relationship-building phase from Zero Seconds to Sign-up. Putting thought into what happens after sign-up will make a noticeable difference to your bottom line: imagine the uplift in revenue if only 1 percent of your after sign-up churn converted to paying customers? What would the impact be if the 1 percent were 10 percent? Paying attention to what happens in the First 48 Hours after your potential buyer signs on is the single most crucial element to optimize in the overall customer journey.

Anxieties at First 48 Hours

At the First 48-Hour milestone (Figure 2.35), you have successfully alleviated most of the anxieties that your site visitor has had, as evidenced by the fact that they chose to Sign-up. The only fears that you have to manage at this stage are ones related to ease of use and delivery of quick wins:

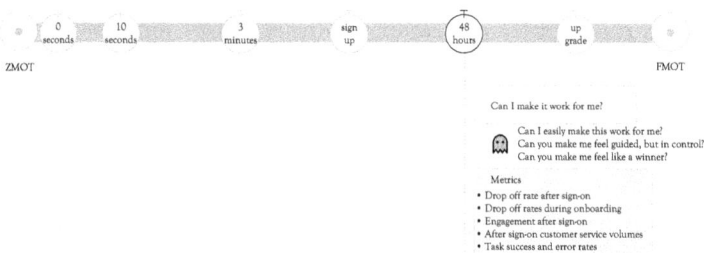

Figure 2.35 The First 48 Hours milestone of the ADORE process™

1. Can I easily make this work for me?
2. Can you make me feel guided but in control?
3. Can you make me feel like a winner?

Remember that the First 48 Hours after Sign-up, you hand over control of the customer experience to your customer. They are in complete control, and while they have made the active commitment to try your product, they are still humans using your product in the context of their busy day. Your product needs to be easy to get started with and deliver a quick win—in doing so, you will extinguish residual anxieties and unblock the pathway toward the upgrade or buying moment.

Common Causes of Issues

The best way to identify issues at the First 48 Hours milestone is to monitor engagement levels after a designated sign-up event. The sign-up could be to your newsletter, to a free trial of your product, to a 30-day paid trial, to a demo, to a fully refundable purchase of wardrobe upgrades. The First 48 Hours milestone principles apply to every moment in your digital space where you ask for an exchange of value.

To spot issues on your digital footprint at the First 48 Hours milestone, monitor the following:

1. High drop off rates after sign-up
2. High drop off rates during onboarding or incomplete onboarding
3. Low engagement rates after sign-up
4. High customer service enquiry volumes connected to onboarding
5. If you are tracking task success rates: low task success or high error rates

Churn, Loss, or Low Engagement After Sign-Up

High drop off rates after sign-up and during onboarding, coupled with low engagement rates after sign-up, are good indicators that your First 48 Hours milestone is not optimized. These metrics will typically come from your Google Analytics or marketing automation tools like Hubspot or Pardot. Unlike the metrics in the previous milestones, these will require some explicit setting up in your tool of choice. This will usually be a piece of code that you paste from the tool or Google Analytics into a specific element on your web page, such as a CTA button inside your web or mobile app. In most cases, your web developer should know how to get this set up.

High Customer Enquiry Volumes During Onboarding

A high volume of customer enquiries related to onboarding or getting started with your product is both a red flag and a terrific gift. If you have customers who have signed up and are willing to place a call or engage in a chat with you, they are incredibly keen to engage with you. Use their queries as a guiding light to what needs to be improved in the onboarding process to render their questions obsolete.

A separate team in your business may track the customer enquiry data. If this is the case, I highly recommend creating a system for sharing high-level data about customer enquiries back into the product team to inform the design and development of your digital presence. You'll get more practical tips on how to do this in Part III.

Low Task Success Rates or High Task Error Rates

Task success rates are not usually tracked automatically. Your website may have elements that are proxies for task success, such as clicking on a particular button to advance to the next step of the onboarding process. These are a good way to collect data on how your customers are engaging with your site, although ideally, task success and task error rates are collected by observing how your customers use your product.

You can conduct easy observational studies using simple tools like a screen recorder or platforms such as Validately or Usability Testing. Setting up a system for regular, small-scale usability tests will have enormous payoffs for your product team. The worksheets at the end of this chapter will help you get started, as will the video lesson on Usability Testing.

How to Fix Issues

The most common cause of issues at the First 48 Hours milestone can all be traced back to one single reason, that being, the time to the first win after sign-up is too long. Whether your onboarding sequence or the perceptions of value are unclear, you can resolve most of the issues at this milestone by mapping out an effortless pathway to the first win. You can achieve this by focusing on:

1. Simplifying the customer journey to the first win
2. Aligning the first win with a perceived value point

Simplify the Customer Journey to the First Win

After sign-up, churn is most often caused by a failure to engage and delight the customer in the first stages after committing to trying out your brand. Lack of engagement can typically be traced to the absence of a straight line to a first win. The first win can be simple: successfully connecting your accounts in a budgeting app or setting up your clients in a job scheduling tool.

To simplify your customer journey or onboarding process, you can lean on best practice strategies that a good UX agency will help you to implement. For best results, these should be tested in the field with real customers, ideally using observational research methods. You can use the worksheets at the end of this chapter to get you started.

Align the First Win With a Perceived Value Point

To maximize your after sign-up retention rates, align your first win with a customer value point. For example, if one of the key reasons that customers use your app is to schedule new jobs quickly, make this the straight line on your onboarding process. Your app may have lots of other functions, but leave these to be discovered by the customer in their own time. The sense of the first win will encourage them to explore, and as soon as they start exploring, they effectively take ownership of the process. If you can get your customers to this point, you have succeeded at the First 48 Hours milestone. The worksheets from the previous chapter will help you identify where your customers' main value points lie. Use these to create a value matrix for your offering (low–high value vs low–high willingness to pay). The worksheets in this chapter will help you get started.

How to Measure Success

The following metrics can measure success at the First 48 Hours milestone:

1. Drop off rate after sign-up
2. Drop off rates during your onboarding process
3. Engagement after sign-up
4. After sign-up customer service enquiry volumes
5. Task success and error rates

Case Study: How a Few Simple UX Changes Increased Monthly Net Payer Gain by 138 Percent for PocketSmith (Figure 2.36)

The results   48 hours

138%	70% E-mail	22% Increase
Increase in	engagement rates	in customer
net payers	after sign-up	retention

Figure 2.36 First 48 Hours case study results

The Challenge

PocketSmith is a fast-growing fintech focused on helping individuals manage their finances. The PocketSmith team had great systems and measures and prided themselves on being objective and data-driven in their product development. They knew that they had nailed their marketing, their brand identity and style resonated with their target audience, and that their product was loved by the customers who made it through their onboarding process. The challenge for them was that while 90 percent of paying customers were active in the first month after signing up, 44 percent of customers were inactive in the second and were therefore more likely to churn. The opportunity cost of these churned customers was high.

The Approach

PocketSmith targeted their product to an audience that they describe as "makers"—a cohort of intelligent, curious, and expansive creators who loved learning new things. The team was attracting the right audience to their website and could not figure out why many were losing interest right after the Sign-up milestone. They expanded their educational material, upped the volume of blogs and information resources, and still had no tangible shifts in the after Sign-up churn rates. Their breakthrough came when the team realized that although their audience loved learning, the onboarding process was not the right time to engage in this education. So instead of educating, they shifted their focus to enabling—removing all resistance from the onboarding process, both in-app and in their e-mail marketing campaigns in the week after Sign-up. Their first e-mail was rewritten as a short and friendly welcome message, which was then followed by an e-mail with a succinct quick start guide to help with onboarding. As a result, more users engaged with the onboarding e-mail—from 58 percent, to consistently over 70 percent (Figure 2.37).

The team identified another source of churn, which correlated with a billing quirk in their system. The backend system that processed payments was queuing transactions and processing them in batches. This resulted in a 24-hour delay between upgrades to a paid plan, allowing some users to downgrade to free before the charge. The team made changes to process the payments for new subscriptions instantly, resulting in an increase in conversion rates from 30 to 37 percent.

We can infer from this that having some skin in the game encourages users to stick around to invest the time in managing their money!
—Jason Leong, CEO PocketSmith

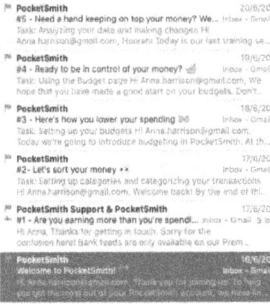

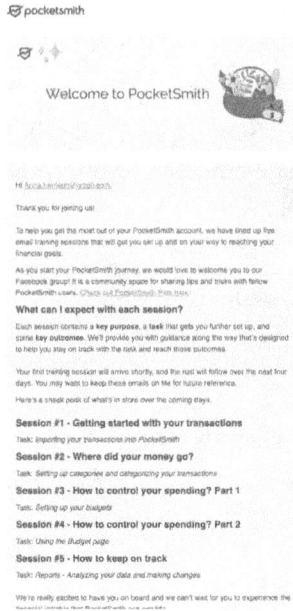

Figure 2.37 PocketSmith's original e-mails invited newly signed-up users to engage in "five e-mail training sessions." Taking away the heaviness of this workload increased engagement rates

A third refinement was an update to the billing e-mails notifying a customer that their payment details needed to be updated. While they technically worked, the designs of the e-mails still reflected PocketSmith's old brand. When this was updated, along with clearer subject lines and copy stating the reason for the payment did not go through, the team saw a 22 percent increase in customer resubscriptions.

These customers were letting their PocketSmith subscriptions lapse simply because the messaging did not inspire trust and had insufficient information—not because they did not love the PocketSmith product.

Why It Worked

The changes made by PocketSmith in the customer journey for the First 48 Hours after Sign-up worked as they directly triggered a number of decision shortcuts. Simplifying the language used in the onboarding e-mails took away the perception that getting started with PocketSmith would be hard and require training. Removing obstacles made the desired behavior easier for the new customers.

The immediacy of billing had a positive effect on retention for two main reasons. The first is that it closed the deal on ownership—seeing a charge to your card plus an acknowledgment in your inbox provides a sense of urgency to get started using the tool you have subscribed to. Once customers began using PocketSmith, completed onboarding, and got their first win, they were highly likely to continue using PocketSmith. The second reason this change worked is that there was a direct connection between the payment and the need to use the tool now.

Updating the copy in the e-mails from "training sessions" to "easy steps" immediately lightened the perceived load of completing the onboarding process. This was a more complex issue to identify, as at face value, the target audience were people who loved learning. The misconception was that they wanted an education during the onboarding process. When reverting to first principles about buying behaviors (Part I), the team formed the hypothesis that they were failing to the power of inertia. Decoupling the two journeys, namely onboarding and education, simplified the perception of engaging with PocketSmith.

Apply It in Your Business

To improve your First 48 Hours retention rates, look for the following signals and opportunities in your business:

1. Find the moment after the Sign-up milestone where you are losing your audience. The easiest way to do this is to set up a simple observational user test—I guarantee that the few hours you invest in this will pay dividends. Use the worksheets in this chapter to get started.
2. Create a short path to the first win after the Sign-up milestone. This is important as it confirms for your customer that you are as you promised, that is easy to work with and easy to use.
    (a) Start with your points of failure
    (b) Overlay the points of perceived value
    (c) Draw a straight line to connect there
    (d) If your product is "complex," use sensible defaults in the onboarding process to shorten the path to the first win. Remember that you don't have to provide a short path to every win—you only need a short path to one win.

3. Review the language in your onboarding and associated e-mail flow. Reduce the perceived difficulty of getting started by:

   (a) Limiting the list of things to do to at most three.

   (b) Removing options from e-mails. If you tell me that I can watch a video, read a blog, sign up for a demo, chat with customer service, or call sales support to help me on board, I will be immediately overwhelmed. Split these into separate e-mails.

   (c) Replacing words like "education" or "training sessions" with lighter, more achievable things like "three steps."

4. If your product is complex, engage a great UX designer to help you deconstruct your onboarding process into a lighter touch sequence, making use of sensible defaults. Remember that your onboarding does not have to get your user started with every feature you offer— only with a small set of the most valuable features. The rest can be configured with subsequent onboarding sequences as needed.

Summary

The First 48 Hours ADORE milestone is your future customer's first real taste of how your offering will make their life better. If you are selling a SaaS product, this is the onboarding process and pathway to a first "win." If you are selling shoes or bicycles, this is the unboxing and first "wow" that comes with using your product. The First 48 Hours is typically the moment that is most worth investing in, as it leads to the biggest return on investments (ROI) on your marketing spend. Typically, measures of success at this milestone are metrics related to after Sign-on retention and churn rates. After Sign-on customer enquiries and task success rates can also be a proxy for measuring effectiveness at the First 48 Hours. If you succeed at this milestone, the next step is a foregone conclusion.

Upgrade

The Moment of Truth

Introduction: Do You Make My Life Better?

This chapter will show you how to:

1. Improve your reengagement rates
2. Decrease your churn rates
3. Improve the ratio of sign-ups to upgrades (to paid)
4. Improve your revenue by selling more, more often

In Part I, we distilled why anyone buys any product or service, experience, or offering down to one single principle—we buy because it makes our life better. The previous milestones in the ADORE process™ have laid out the conditions that you need to create to get your site visitor to commit to your brand. We now need to add the elements to make them stay and pay.

My parents are both mathematicians, highly practical, and very much old school when it comes to the subtle art of self-promotion. Their view is that great work speaks for itself, and therefore, there is no need for self-promotion. Q.E.D.

The problem with this approach is that it does not work. It does not work in the workplace, it does not work in a romantic relationship, and it does not work on Internet Street (John 2021; de Botton 2017; Taniguchi 2021). The fact is that if you don't tell, and then remind, the people who matter about how it is that you make their life better, they might just forget. Not because they don't value the relationship, but simply because they are thinking about 35,000 other things.

It is not enough to deliver a quality offering and to get someone through all the ADORE milestones to the point of sign-up and engagement. To get them to buy, and rebuy, from you, you need to create an authentic yet systematic way to remind your customers exactly how you make their life better (Figure 2.38). To be authentic, your reminder system should be decoupled from your billing cycles.

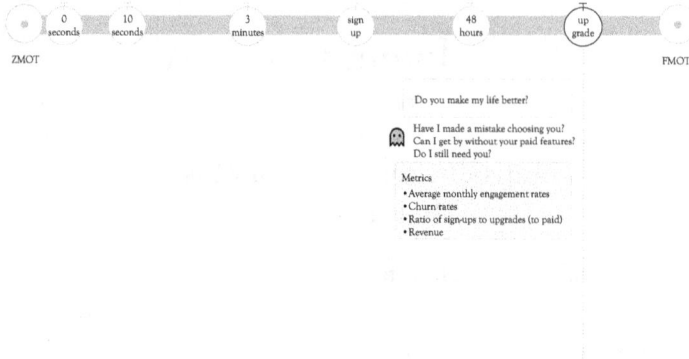

Figure 2.38 *The Upgrade milestone of the ADORE Process*™

Anxieties at Upgrade

To get your customer through the final ADORE milestone, the upgrade moment where they buy or rebuy your offering, you need to address the following anxieties regularly:

1. Have I made a mistake in choosing you?
2. Can I get by without your paid/premium features?
3. Do I still need you?

If you can alleviate these fears, you have successfully optimized your digital presence and created a system for scaling lasting relationships between site visitors and your brand.

Common Causes of Issues

The following signs will give you an indication that your Upgrade milestone can be improved:

1. Your month-on-month reengagement rates are low.
2. Your churn rates are high.

3. The ratio of sign-ups to upgrades (to paid) is low.

4. Your rebuy rates are low or zero.

5. Your revenue rates are below your expectations.

Low Reengagement Rates or High Churn Rates

Low reengagement rates and high churn rates often indicate that your product is too hard to use and/or does not deliver on expected value. It is a good idea to determine which of these causes is driving your particular reengagement or churn. The best way to do this is simply to ask a handful of your customers. While not statistically significant, once you notice a pattern in the responses, you can deploy the questions to a broader audience as a survey to confirm or refute the initial hypothesis.

If the causes are related to usability, refer back to the notes in the Sign-up chapter and set up some usability studies to understand the failure points. Alternately, work with a good UX agency to identify and rectify the issues.

If, on the other hand, your product fails to deliver on expected value, you may need to step back and reassess your overall business strategy, with an eye on:

1. Are you overpromising or misleading your buyers during the earlier ADORE milestones? Your long-term reputation is in danger if this is the case.

2. Are you solving a problem that your target audience wants solved? For example, Juicero quite famously created a beautifully designed juicer, only to discover that they were outcompeted by a pair of scissors.

3. Is the reason you set up your business a decade ago still relevant to the target audience? Have you missed a critical inflection point and failed to stay at the head of the curve?

4. Is your target audience ready for your offering, or do they need to change their existing behavior first? The insurance industry is an excellent example of a sector that could be ingesting insights from modern technologies yet still relies on old fashioned clipboards and paper-based forms (quite literally).

Understanding the exact reasons your offering may fail to sell at the rate you desire is a necessary first step. Once you identify the real cause, refer back to the corresponding milestone in the ADORE process™ for an approach on how to remedy the issue.

Ratio of Sign-Up to Upgrade Is Low

Poor Upgrade milestone performance is often caused when too much value is given away in your product's free or trial version. If the Signed-up customer can solve their problem well enough without upgrading, they won't need to upgrade. Businesses in the early phase of growth often undercut themselves and give away too much value in an effort to grow their customer numbers more quickly. This may be a great strategy if you are VC funded and can sustain years of losses. However, even in this case, there is a danger that as your customer base grows, they will become increasingly anchored to your free offering. Taking this away later or changing what you give away for free will activate several decision short-cuts, exacerbating the perceived loss and anchoring customers to what was there. Tiny MCE, the once open-source product that powered the **B**, *I*, <u>U</u> buttons on most major websites, took over a decade to transition their product from a free, open-source offering to a paid cloud subscription model. The process was not easy, and there were moments where they lost many loyal fans along the way. The lesson here is—if you note low reengagement and high churn rates after Sign-on, tune your model early. You will increase revenue and create a smoother transition to loyalty than if you leave it for later.

Rebuy Rates Are Low or Zero

The case of zero return buyers or close to zero rebuys can, in exceptional circumstances, be an indicator of product success. Online dating sites, orthodontists, wedding dress retailers, and houses are terrific examples of once in a lifetime (perhaps aspirationally) buys. If your offering falls into this category, then invert the rebuy metrics and strive to get yours close to zero. Successfully solving a problem is an excellent opportunity to create a large and loyal following of brand advocates. If this applies to you, there are some great tips in the last chapter on the Referral, or RIP milestone.

For everyone else, zero repeat buys are an issue worth investigating. The approach you could take is similar to that for low ratio of customer upgrades. First, seek to understand why, and then revisit the ADORE process™ with a renewed focus on solving that need.

Revenue Rates Below Expectations

Finally, if your metrics in this section are all good, that is, your ratio of postsign-up engagement is great, and your Upgrade rates are great, and you are still not making the revenue that you want to be making, then you may need to step outside of your digital presence to resolve the issue.

It could be that your pricing model is an order of magnitude out of sync with where the market is, something that can happen if you have been in business for over a decade. It could be that your offering is using an outdated technology (either virtual or in the actual production process) that is creating inefficiencies and an opportunity for competitors to outmaneuver you.

How to Fix Issues

Improve Your UX

In the first instance of high churn or low engagement rates, revisit the Sign-up milestone, which focused on onboarding. Issues with onboarding are a specific case of more general issues with usability, or UX and UI. As with onboarding, the best way to identify UX and UI issues is to create a series of observational user tests and use the insights gained as a starting point. Personal experience and general product industry guidelines indicate that you will get breakthrough insights with five participants—as long as you make an effort to structure your user tests or experiments well (Harrison 2020a).

Repackage Your Offering

If you find yourself competing against free versions of your own product, it may be worthwhile deconstructing your offering and repackaging it to align with your customers' value points. Refer back to the Sign-up chapter, and revisit your worksheets to get ideas on how to get started with this task.

Align Perceived Value With Rebuy Moments

Failure to upgrade or generate rebuys has different solutions depending on the reasons for the issue. If the problem is caused by a lack of perceived value, you will need to reexamine your pricing model and realign your offering to match the points where customers get the most value. Refer to the Sign-up chapter for details and worksheets.

If you have a case of zero rebuys, you may be in a category of offerings that solve a particular problem for the buyer, in other words, the zero rebuy is an indication of success. If your product falls into this category, leverage the situation to create an army of active ambassadors for your brand. This is discussed in the last ADORE milestone—Recommend, or RIP.

Consider a Strategic Merger

In the last case, if you suspect that your metrics are all performing well and your revenue is still below desired levels, look for opportunities to merge or partner with competitors or adjacent businesses. A well-executed strategic merger can often revive and accelerate business growth and expand the offering to new target markets. Facebook's acquisitions of Instagram and WhatsApp allowed Facebook to capture the attention of markets they were missing out on: Instagram gave them access to a younger demographic, while WhatsApp opened the doors to connecting with a more global audience.

How to Measure Success

The following metrics can measure success at the Upgrade milestone:

1. Average monthly engagement rates
2. Churn rates
3. Ratio of sign-ups to upgrades (to paid)
4. Revenue

Case Study: How Grammarly Uses a Weekly Newsletter as a Clever Reminder of Their Value to Maintain Engagement (Figure 2.39)

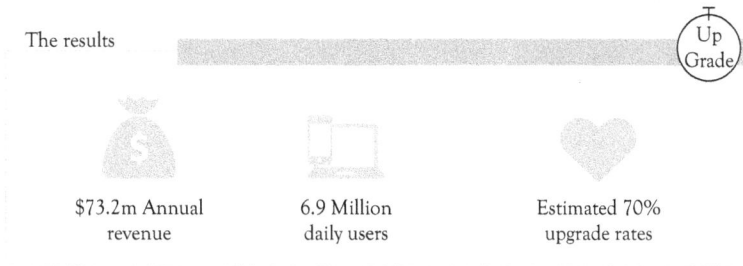

Figure 2.39 Upgrade case study results

The Challenge

In this case study, we depart from analyzing growing brands and look at a household name that has created a unique system for converting their digital relationships from Sign-up to Upgrade and rebuy. The Grammarly business story is quite interesting, as they started as a paid enterprise offering, and over a decade, grew into a freemium consumer product ("How Grammarly Quietly Grew Its Way to 6.9 Million Daily Users in 9 Years" 2017). Although Grammarly is now a household name, they continue to put tremendous effort into ensuring that they remind their users of their value. Their consistent, personalized, and evolving system for doing this is a pivotal component of their incredibly high retention rates.

The Approach

Grammarly's headline in Google is "Grammarly: Free Online Writing Assistant." They draw you into using their tool through a zero risk, simple installation process of the free version of their product as a browser add-on. Grammarly activates a weekly summary of Grammarly Insights sent to you by e-mail as soon as you sign up. The weekly update provides you with basic stats about how many words you checked, how many mistakes Grammarly corrected for you, and how you compared to other people using Grammarly—they have turned e-mail writing into a competitive sport. Each e-mail is also a subtle reminder of the value you are leaving on the table by not upgrading, in the form of "mistakes that we found, that you can unlock by upgrading." Their system creates the ultimate FOMO (fear of missing out) and makes it effortless to upgrade to get the big reveal (Figure 2.40).

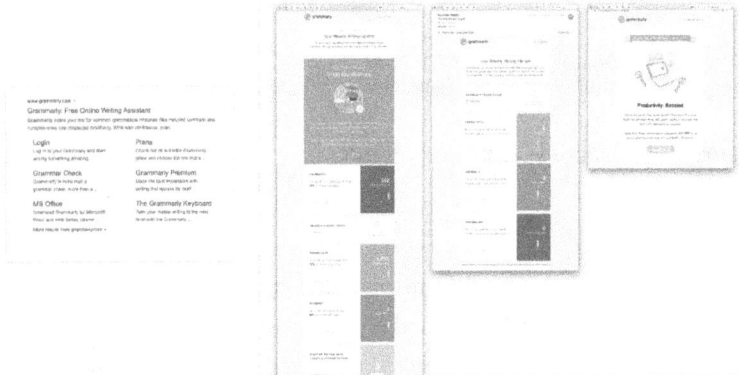

Figure 2.40 *Grammarly e-mails take you on a journey of deepening commitment while creating a strong sense of* FOMO

As you use Grammarly, you are introduced to extended useful features in-situ and through their weekly e-mail updates. The feature revelations are relevant to the way you use Grammarly and so are extremely useful. Grammarly has successfully turned their e-mail marketing campaigns into a trusted relationship.

Why It Worked

Grammarly's strategy to convert users into paying customers is one of the best in market. It has helped them double their revenue and active users each year since the business started in 2008. Their approach is worth deconstructing, understanding, and applying in your business.

The approach taken by Grammarly works because:

1. The resistance to getting started is almost zero. The browser extension is free and easy to install, and you get immediate utility.
2. The points you are invited to upgrade are connected to the moments you have the highest perceived value from the app. If you use the free version and load in a new 4,000-word document, you're actively and heavily invested in getting that document checked. That's the perfect moment to ask the user to upgrade: you have used your free quota, upgrade, and never miss another mistake.
3. The weekly e-mails from Grammarly reinforce the value that the app is delivering to you each week—the newsletters are personalized with your actual statistic and only contain offers to upgrade at points where you will receive value from the upgrade. In addition, the newsletters are fun! You receive reports that are lightly competitive and encouraging: "You were more accurate than 96 percent of Grammarly users this week" (I am awesome!); "You were more productive than 71 percent of Grammarly users this week" (I am winning!); "Grammarly Premium found three additional mistakes that you could have corrected—Upgrade now" (instant FOMO).

Apply It in Your Business

Grammarly has evolved a perfect balance between utility in their offering and a reminder of their utility—or how they make your life better—through their personalized weekly newsletter delivery. While they set the gold standard, you can learn from their example and apply it in your own business:

1. Map out your end-to-end product usage journey, and mark:
   (a) Rates of engagement at key points
   (b) Perceived value at key points
2. Map out your value matrix by aligning your value points with your target audience's willingness to pay. Overlay your rates of engagement over the matrix.
3. Note whether the points of engagement, points of value, and payment points align, and if they do not, adjust your process.
4. Use the ADORE process™ to optimize the journey on your website and ensure that your value is supported through regular communications via e-mail, socials, or whatever channel your target audience uses to engage with you.

Summary

The Upgrade ADORE milestone is the maintenance phase of the relationship between your buyer and your brand. Even if your product or service is spectacular, and there is no one else like you, your buyer will still need occasional reminders of exactly how it is that you make their life better. Putting these systems in place in an authentic way will lengthen the average lifetime value of your average customer. The next and final step is to leverage the great work that you have done in building strong relationships with your buyers, and using the momentum to drive recommended traffic to your website.

Recommend, or RIP

Introduction: Do You Make Me a Hero?

This chapter will show you how to:

1. Improve your ratio of repeat buyers
2. Address a high or increasing volume of inactive accounts
3. Decrease your churn rates
4. Improve your Net Promoter Score (NPS)

Most businesses think the customer journey finishes when the purchase is made. Thinking about what happens next has the power to elevate you simply because your competitors will not be thinking about this forgotten part of the overall customer experience (Figure 2.41).

Figure 2.41 The recommend or RIP milestone of the ADORE process™

In Part I, we looked at the financial benefits of having a loyal customer base, both in terms of increased revenue and resistance to downturns. We looked at the model of experience, in particular how the recommendation of others is the most powerful impetus to buy. Most businesses may know this yet fail to use it.

Product design is still an evolving field and one that has matured over the last decade. Five years ago, it was rare to walk into a product team with efficient systems in place to connect feedback from various departments, such as customer service, marketing, design, and development, back into the product team. The data was often collected, however, the feedback loop was not in place. Although it is more common, businesses that do this remain in the minority. Similarly, relatively few businesses conduct proactive exit interviews to interrogate and understand the reasons why customers leave. Building these feedback loops and taking an active interest in why your customers leave (or ghost) will give you insights that you can use to create a sustainable competitive advantage. Businesses like Amazon do this incredibly well. Their connectivity and information sharing across the supply chain is rewarded with lasting loyalty: around 33 percent of all Americans are Amazon Prime subscribers and treat Amazon as their ZMOT—it is the first place they go to check for new items, price compare, and buy online. The flow-on of loyalty, recommendations, and consistent rebuys are an integral factor in the company's revenue projections for 2025, which are predicted to double from the current highs (Arcieri 2021). A very different example, Expensify grew its business to more than $100 million in annual recurring revenue and millions of users with a staff of 130, a few contractors, and a sales team of zero. They achieved this exclusively through recommendations from existing customers (Heim 2021).

The differential in revenue to a business like Afterpay, Expensify, or the one you are running, from even a small shift in loyalty, is compounded by the flow-on effects of recommendations and reviews by brand advocates. What happens postpurchase affects the expectations, and therefore satisfaction of future customers—and shortens the buying process by eliminating your competitors from the evaluation and research phases (Figure 2.42).

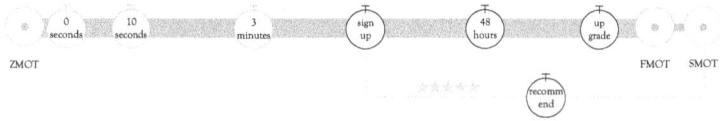

Figure 2.42 A strong recommendation eliminates all other brands from consideration and reduces the evaluation and research periods

Anxieties at Recommend, or RIP

Most people will continue to buy from a brand not only if the brand makes their life better but if the brand makes them a hero. It may seem far-fetched to think that a brand has the power to make one a hero, but remember that on a human level, we all track the sun in 24-hour increments. We all juggle careers, children, ambitions, desires, and fears. The brands that make us heroes are the ones that lead to promotions at work or an elevation in social status with the other soccer mothers. These are the brands that deliver inferred credibility through our association with them or generate positive results for the people to whom we personally recommend the brand. The adage that no "one ever got fired for choosing IBM" is the point of inertia that your brand needs to outcompete to lock in a lasting and rewarding relationship with your buyers. Helping your brand advocate to feel like a hero will overcome the anxiety that people may harbor about putting their reputation on the line in making a recommendation.

Common Causes of Issues

The best way to spot issues at the Recommend, or RIP milestone is to look at the metrics that track repeat buys and your reputation in the marketplace:

1. Your volume of inactive accounts is increasing.
2. Your churn rates are high and increasing.
3. Your NPSs are low, or reviews about your brand on influential websites are poor.

Volume of Inactive Accounts or Churn Is Increasing

Inactive accounts and churn rates are dormant metrics that are easy to overlook. Marketing as a discipline focuses on filling the top of the funnel, and Sales concentrates on deals closed. Customer reengagement or retention is a relatively new role emerging in customer service departments; it is rarely a dedicated role in the product team. These factors contribute to the economic flywheel that fattens the wallets of Google: raise more VC funds, so that you can spend more on marketing, so that 3 percent of these customers will buy once from you, so that you need to find more customers.

If you are fortunate enough to have inactive accounts and customers who churn, use the opportunity as a gift to interrogate why the customers are not buying from you again. Whatever you discover will help you make your digital offering more effective, improving the potential for lasting relationships with new site visitors. The worksheets in the last few chapters will give you some handy pointers to get started.

NPS or Reviews Are Dropping

If your brand reputation is poor in places where your customers leave reviews, your marketing efforts will be undermined. No matter how much budget you pour into attracting new traffic to your website, lackluster reviews will place doubt in your potential buyers' minds and likely turn them away to a competitor. The effects of poor reviews have a very long tail—with consumer brands, the damage can last for years. With industrial brands, the consequences can last for decades. For example, it is common for travelers to avoid airports for decades after having a single bad experience—even if the airport is rebuilt and the issues eliminated, travelers continue to avoid Heathrow as "it is a nightmare" (Harrison 2015). In consumer brands, a bad batch of electronics may lead to a spray of low star ratings from irate customers, such as this review of a Bosch induction cooktop (Figure 2.43). Although the review was posted in 2017, it is enough to place enough doubt in the minds of today's buyers that they turn to a competitor who does not have poor reviews.

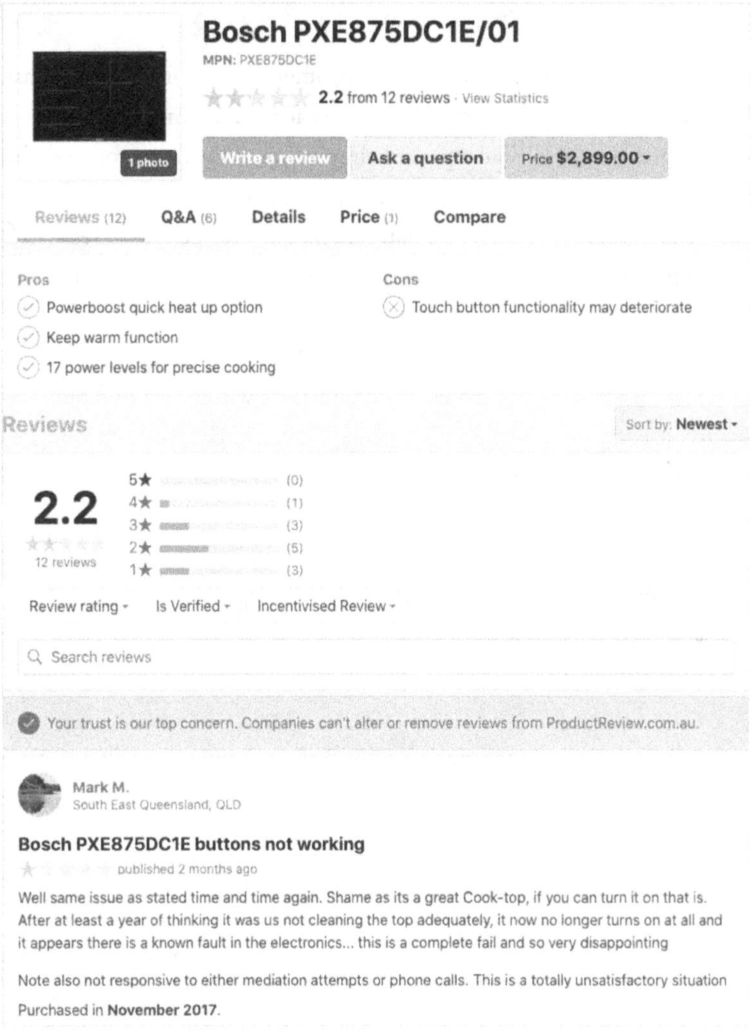

Bosch PXE875DC1E/01
MPN: PXE875DC1E

★★☆☆☆ **2.2** from 12 reviews · View Statistics

| 1 photo | Write a review | Ask a question | Price **$2,899.00** ▾ |

Reviews (12)   **Q&A** (6)   **Details**   **Price** (1)   **Compare**

Pros

⊘ Powerboost quick heat up option
⊘ Keep warm function
⊘ 17 power levels for precise cooking

Cons

⊗ Touch button functionality may deteriorate

Reviews

Sort by: **Newest** ▾

2.2
★★☆☆☆
12 reviews

5★		(0)
4★		(1)
3★		(3)
2★		(5)
1★		(3)

Review rating ▾   Is Verified ▾   Incentivised Review ▾

🔍 Search reviews

✓ Your trust is our top concern. Companies can't alter or remove reviews from ProductReview.com.au.

Mark M.
South East Queensland, QLD

Bosch PXE875DC1E buttons not working

★☆☆☆☆   published 2 months ago

Well same issue as stated time and time again. Shame as its a great Cook-top, if you can turn it on that is. After at least a year of thinking it was us not cleaning the top adequately, it now no longer turns on at all and it appears there is a known fault in the electronics... this is a complete fail and so very disappointing

Note also not responsive to either mediation attempts or phone calls. This is a totally unsatisfactory situation

Purchased in **November 2017**.

Figure 2.43 Poor reviews on third-party websites will impact the credibility of your brand

How to Fix Issues

Fixing leaks at this stage of the process will give you the most significant payoffs. It is far more expensive to attract a new customer and invest in walking them through the entire ADORE process™ than to retain a customer who has already committed to your brand.

Understand Why Customers Leave You

A great way to gain insights into why customers leave you is simply to ask them. To do this, you can use the strategies for conducting observational user research (refer to Sign-up) and simply reach out to customers who have left and ask them why. It's essential to listen to what is said and the words that are used, as there is a natural tendency for people to resist giving negative feedback. In these cases, a hesitation or a pause can be your breakthrough insight.

Once you have collected the data, refrain from jumping straight into action mode to fix all the issues. Each customer will have a different reason for leaving you, and fundamentally, you cannot be everything to everyone. A simple strategy to approach the analysis of feedback is to partition your interviewees into three buckets:

1. Low-value customers
2. Mid-value customers
3. High-value customers

Look for patterns that emerge within these groups, and then action accordingly.

Low-Value Customers

Consider whether it is worth responding to the needs of your lowest value customers pragmatically. Do a simple cost–benefit analysis and be honest about whether servicing these customers is financially beneficial. Consider also whether these customers genuinely represent your target audience, and if not, then your best option may be to learn to say no to this group and refer them on to someone else.

Mid-Value Customers

Inactive accounts in the mid-value customer range are worth focusing on, as these customers contribute enough margin and are part of your target audience. Understand why they are dis-engaging and create a strategy to reengage this group through targeted marketing activations. Grammarly sends out e-mails to encourage you to reengage when they notice a period of inactivity. The e-mails are positive and easy to action—they invite you to take a small step only. Check that your messaging in this category is appropriate. For example, a customer that has not been engaged will not be wanting to upgrade to your premium offering. Reengage by following the ADORE process™ from the start and reenergize the relationship step by step.

High-Value Customers

Your high-value customers' feedback should be considered with priority, although again, refrain from being reactive. Take time to understand why high-value customers are leaving you. It can be very tempting to do everything that a large customer wants, especially in the earlier growth phases of your business. If what is requested aligns with your business strategy and vision, action it with priority. If it does not, you will need to weigh up the pros and cons and consider consciously putting measures in place to diversify your reliance on any one large customer.

Address Credibility Breaches Proactively

If your brand has a bad run and is slammed with poor reviews, acknowledge and provide a remedy publicly. Recall from Part I that you can use information to moderate expectations to turn a negative experience into a positive one. Let's say Bosch releases a series of induction cooktops that have faulty buttons, which attracts unfavorable reviews on third-party websites. It will serve Bosch to address this transparently, provide a remedy, and a commitment to resolution. For example, we know that this model was faulty, we have addressed the problem, and if you have one of these defective induction cooktops, we will replace it for you. Addressing the issue proactively will strengthen the brand in the consumers' eyes, whereas simply ignoring the poor reviews creates a long tail of diminished brand credibility.

How to Measure Success

Your brand is positively affected by the flow-on effects of strong brand relationships if you note the following metrics:

1. Ratio of repeat buyers is strong.
2. Your inactive account volume decreases.
3. Your churn rates are low.
4. Your NPSs are high.
5. You have great reviews and recommendations on third-party websites.

Case Study: How Intuto Repositioned Their Twenty-Year-Old Brand by Listening to Loyal Customers

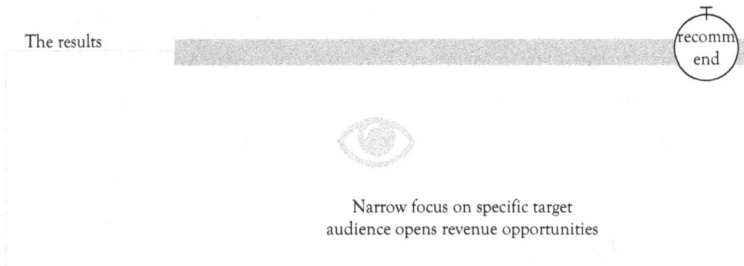

The results

recommend

Narrow focus on specific target
audience opens revenue opportunities

Figure 2.44 Recommend, or RIP case study results

The Challenge

Intuto was an early pioneer in online education, creating a learning platform and content conversion service in 2000. Early success with several iconic enterprise customers allowed Intuto to focus on their growing business. Early success led to an anchoring of the platform with existing customers and a delay in responding to the changes in the online learning market. Intuto was facing the challenge of repositioning themselves to regain their market lead in what had become a crowded market. As an additional challenge, the team had some legacy services that they were running as loss leaders. They were also unsure how to introduce changes to their pricing model with grace and respect for their long-standing, loyal customer base.

The Approach

Intuto sensed that they would need to specialize their services and focus on a niche target audience to regain a strong foothold in the market. Intuto's biggest asset was the pool of loyal customers that the business had serviced for over two decades. They leaned on their trusted relationships to gain insights into what their customers valued the most about their services. The plan was to use these insights to find an online education sector that was underserviced yet had enough urgency and cash flow to make the narrowing of target audience profitable for the business.

Intuto began by partitioning all of their existing clients into three segments: high-value, mid-value, and low-value. Within each segment, they further divided their customers by sector. Intuto placed calls to representative clients to discover what they valued most about the brand and what they thought they were paying for. Intuto paired these insights with research into the broader trends in online learning.

The team applied the ADORE process™ consecutively to a series of experiments of increasing commitment (on their part) and increasing acceptance (on their clients' part). The systematic approach of experimentation and validation de-risked the change process for Intuto. The arc of their progress looked a little like this:

1. Intuto triangulated the market research and customer interview data and identified the health sector as a target market that was behind the adoption curve in online learning yet had a high need to do so (compliance, safety, efficiency of training, reporting).
2. With the health sector in mind, they looked at their database of existing clients to see if they had any existing strong relationships. Going into the exercise, Intuto had thought of themselves as servicing the hospitality industry and a few others. As it turned out, they already had a good number of health equipment manufacturers on their books, they simply had not noticed or focused on these clients separately.

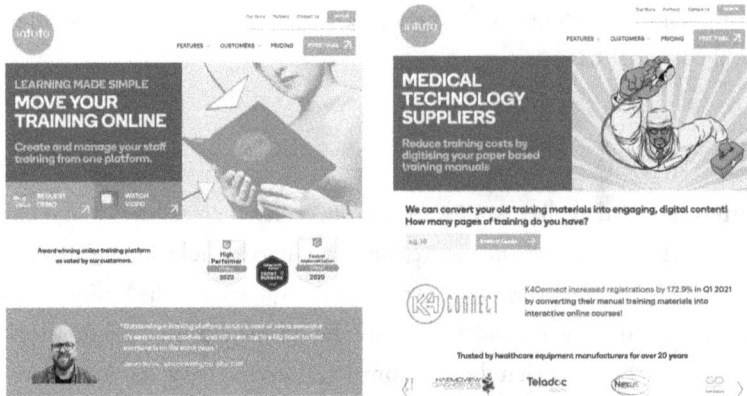

Figure 2.45 Intuto analyzed its portfolio of customers, creating a specialized offering for their high-value customers in the medical field

3. Before changing anything too radically on their website, they soft-launched a content conversion service and bespoke pricing model at a health conference. The offer they had constructed resonated with their target audience.

4. They created a new landing page targeting the health sector. They were careful to follow the ADORE process™ to ensure that the value proposition, trust and credibility, and invitation to take action (through an instant content conversion calculator) were optimally positioned on the new page.

5. As a final step, Intuto launched an e-mail marketing campaign targeting health equipment manufacturers to drive awareness of their new offer.

The journey to becoming exclusively focused on the health sector will take a couple of years to execute as the business continues to service existing clients in other sectors. By bringing a more focused offering to market for a particular audience, Intuto can refine the specialized offering and adjust the pricing model without alienating the existing customers.

Why It Worked

The approach was at first counterintuitive—a strategy for growth based on eliminating market segments. However, when Intuto completed the first part of the analysis, they found that they were spending most of their resources servicing clients that simply did not have the cash flow to pay for their higher-margin offerings. Removing the low-value customers from their growth plans freed Intuto to consider how to better serve the customers that were in the high-value bucket.

The second part of the analysis revealed that the health sector was in general underserviced by specialist online learning platforms. In numbers, majority of Intuto's customers fell in the low-value buckets—and by chance, the customers in their high-value segments were mainly in the health sector already. The overlap gave Intuto the ability to interrogate these customers further, extract their perceived points of value, and design up a series of experiments targeting a narrower market segment.

The conversations with customers in the health sector revealed that one of the main pain points for this group lay in converting existing pdf or PowerPoint-based training materials into online formats. Intuto had decades of experience in solving for this and now could charge market rates for the services. The majority of their existing clients did not have the capacity to pay for this service, and Intuto was therefore running it as a loss leader to generate goodwill. To the right market segment, the same offering had gained value.

Having gained confidence that their narrower target audience was not only viable but presented a market opportunity for Intuto to take the lead once again, the company revised its pricing model. The simplified pricing model was extended with their content creation services as an add-on available to premium subscribers.

Apply It in Your Business

The customers who already use your services, and the ones that stop using your service, are two largely untapped sources of valuable data. A handful of phone calls to a specific set of customers can reveal more insights than terabytes of data collected by Google—I'm not suggesting that one is better than the other, but simply highlight that your answers could lie hidden with the customers you already have, and the phone calls you can easily make.

To apply the strategies that worked for Intuto in your business, start by segmenting your existing customers into three buckets:

1. Low-value customers
2. Mid-value customers
3. High-value customers

Evaluate objectively whether the low-value customers are worthwhile servicing, and if not, make a conscious decision not to grow in that direction. Focus on your high-value customers and look for patterns:

1. Are there common pain points?
2. Are there common sectors?
3. Do you understand why high-value customers may have left you?
4. Do you understand why high-value customers remain loyal?

Typically, understanding the core values and creating a marketing and growth strategy that focuses on high-value clients will grow your revenue faster than a strategy of diluting attention to service a broader customer base.

However, a word of caution—the decision to focus on a more specific target audience may temporarily lower your performance metrics. Your experience in your business and the industry will give you the information that you need to know whether the dips are temporary or whether the move was a mistake that ought to be reversed. A great way to test the market is the way that Intuto did—by vetting the new offering with the right audience, standing up new targeted landing pages and driving traffic to those. The great thing about digital is that you can experiment with different relationship models simultaneously, adjust, refine, and continue doing more of what works for your business. Using the ADORE process™ will give you the systematic foundation to efficiently construct, execute, and evaluate these experiments.

Summary

The Recommend, or RIP ADORE milestone puts in place the final step of the brand loyalty flywheel, closing the loop and setting "perpetual brand loyalty" described in Part I into motion. This milestone considers how existing, lost, and loyal customers interact with the opinions of future buyers to affect your sales long past the current transaction. Simple strategies that you can use to gain a marked competitive advantage and future-proof your revenue streams were explored.

Part III will show you how to scale the ADORE process™ to get the most out of working with digital agencies and running in-house product teams.

PART III

Applying the ADORE Process

When I started looking into improving our SEO, I was immediately confused and overwhelmed with conflicting information. I spoke to a business development consultant, two different marketing companies, a web developer, a specialist SEO company... every one of them had different ideas about what to do.

—Brian Corff, COO, kindSIGHT Ophthalmology

Getting started is often the hardest part. In *Life in Half a Second*, Michalewicz describes a simple process for getting started on a new and overwhelming assignment—break it down into 10 boxes, and each of those boxes into 10 boxes, and so on, until you arrive at a list of tasks that you can complete in a day. To make it easy to get started with ADORE, you can follow the simple process shown in Figure 3.1.

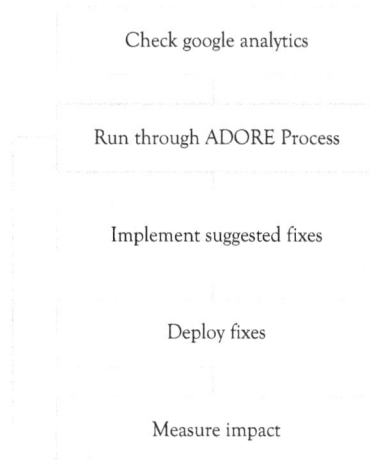

Check google analytics

Run through ADORE Process

Implement suggested fixes

Deploy fixes

Measure impact

Figure 3.1 Getting started with the ADORE Process™ in your business

Start by connecting your digital asset, for example website, to a data collection system such as Google Analytics. There are numerous other options, each with pros, cons, and varying price points. Ensure that you are, at a minimum, collecting these essential metrics:

1. Site visitors and bounce rates
2. Average time on site and number of return visits
3. Ratio of site visitors to sign-ups
4. Postsign-up engagement at 48 hours, one week, and one month
5. Ratio of sign-ups to upgrades
6. Average transaction size

Periodically, run through the steps in the ADORE process™, and note any areas where your metrics have dropped or are lower than your targets. Follow the guidelines in Part II to both understand and fix any issues that you have detected. The fixes described for each ADORE milestone create a sound basis for a program of works for your internal team or external agency. If you are working with external agencies or freelance specialists, you can use the ADORE process™ to measure and track the performance of work delivered by various parties. The following section will give you additional tips on using ADORE to your advantage when working with agencies.

Once the work has been rolled out, be sure to measure the impact a few months down track. If the metrics you are tracking have improved, terrific. If they have not, review the changes that were made and adjust. Note that in most cases, the nature of the work has an experimental component to it. Use the metrics as an objective guide and a baseline for how the changes are performing. Repeat the process each time updates are rolled out.

Working With Agencies and Product Teams

Improvements suggested by applying the ADORE process™ will typically involve changes to your website, your outbound e-mails, or your web or mobile app. Each change will require a different mix of skills or capabilities. This is often the part that poses the biggest challenge to business owners as it is impossible to find one person or agency with all the skills. Outsourcing the work to the wrong type of professional can have adverse effects. Beware of old Maslow's adage of "when all you have is a hammer, everything looks like a nail" (Maslow 1966): a marketing agency will try to solve all problems by increasing always-on marketing spend; a design agency by creating more attractive designs; a development agency by updating the code or replatforming your website. Your win lies in understanding what capabilities are needed to implement the fixes at each stage of the ADORE process™, sending the work to an appropriately skilled team, and using the right metrics to measure the quality and impact of their work (Figure 3.2).

Looking at the distinct stages of the ADORE process™, note that different capabilities are needed to complete work at each stage. Typically, these capabilities are collected together into different types of agencies or a dedicated product team. For example, it is rare to find a mid-tier agency with expertise in all of these areas:

1. Search engine optimization specialist
2. Marketing strategist

ADORE Zero seconds	Search engine optimization specialist marketing strategist	#site visitors
ADORE Ten seconds	Graphic designer UX designer copywriter	#bounce rates
ADORE Three minutes	Content strategist brand strategist UX designer	#time on site #return visitor rates
ADORE Sign-up	Behavioral economist or marketing strategist UX designer web developer	#ratio of visitor to sign-ups
ADORE First 48 Hours	UX designer web developer usability testing specialist	#engagemen rates after sign-up
ADORE Upgrade	Sales pricing specialist UX designer web developer usability testing specialist	#revenue #ratio of re-buy
ADORE Recommend, or RIP	Marketing specialist customer success specialist web developer	#NPS scores #third party ratings

Figure 3.2 Capabilities needed to implement fixes at each stage of the ADORE Process™ and the recommended success metrics to track progress

3. Graphic designer
4. UX designer
5. Copywriter
6. Branding strategist
7. Content strategist
8. Behavioral economist
9. Web developer
10. Usability testing specialist
11. SaaS pricing specialist
12. Customer success specialist

Most agencies tend to group expertise around a narrower set of capabilities:

1. SEO agencies or freelancers (ADORE Zero Seconds)
2. Marketing and branding agencies (ADORE Ten Seconds)
3. Web design agencies (ADORE Three Minutes and Sign-up)
4. UX/UI design agencies (ADORE First 48 Hours and Upgrade)
5. Development agencies (needs will depend on channel, e.g., website or mobile app)

From this perspective, it is easy to see the challenge in delivering a holistic customer experience, particularly one that requires the creation of digital elements, which together serve to evolve the relationship with your next buyer. Even assuming that each agency delivers high-quality work, there is no continuity or accountability when work is handed off between agencies. As a business owner, this leaves you in a vulnerable position: the onus is on you to balance the delivery of an optimized digital presence, and coordinate interrelated work between independent agencies. In the worst case, the agency you hire convinces you that all the issues can be solved using their particular type of hammer.

Regardless of which situation you are in, the compounding challenge in the industry is that agency outcomes are not tied to performance metrics. A web development or web design agency will happily take a monthly retainer, regardless of whether the work they deliver leads to you selling more, more often, or not. This is not because of any deficiencies in any particular agency—it is simply a reflection of the industry's current state. Very few agencies use metrics to measure the effectiveness of their work, and fewer still charge clients based on the performance of work delivered. Effectively, this creates a situation where the work is handed off to agencies, and despite the necessarily experimental and iterative nature of most "fixes" in this space, no one is tracking how well the most recent change is working on the entirety of the brand buyer relationship.

A 2021 Forrester Research report describes the emerging set of tools in the "journey orchestration" genre, which have the potential to address some of the end-to-end data collection issues identified. However, these tools are currently offered at enterprise price points, making them inaccessible outside Fortune 500 organizations. You can use the ADORE process™ to supplement your data collection with the insights that would otherwise be delivered by some of these enterprise tools.

Which Metrics Matter Most?

Last year, I worked with a client who runs a modern, data-centric business and tracks all the right metrics. Their current month's data fit neatly into a 50-page pdf report. Examining the metrics through the ADORE process™ lens allowed us to see what they had been missing month on month. ADORE identified a clear point at which they were leaking revenue, which, when understood, freed them up to make the change—in this case, a few simple UX adjustments resulted in an immediate $50,000 uplift in revenue. The key was in understanding which of their metrics mattered the most.

Product design as a discipline is still relatively young, especially when compared to areas such as sales, marketing, or even software development. In these fields, "success" is readily measured by metrics such as dollars (sales), traffic and leads (marketing), and velocity (software development). However, when it comes to product design, we still often think of it as "art": the beauty of a lovely interaction, a perfect color scheme or style guide, engaging graphics. Think about the last time you were asked to deliver a product design project or engaged an agency to do the same: what metrics were you given as delivery targets? How did you know if the agency you hired did a good job? How did you know if the solution was better than what you had before?

Each metric you collect is an indicator of performance at a specific ADORE milestone.

Knowing which metrics to use to evaluate product design quality will help you build better products and get more value from engagements with agencies. It will also give you an objective way to measure your designers and product team's performance and provide guidance to early career team members.

In the first two parts of this book, you learned the formula for digital brand loyalty and the effect that loyal customers have on all future customers through the power of referrals or personal recommendations.

Let's consider each of the customers in isolation. The likelihood that they will convert into a loyal customer is described by the cumulative effect of each step in the ADORE process™. Different metrics measure success at each of these steps. For example, high bounce rates tell us nothing about whether the pricing model is correct, and newsletter sign-ups do not describe the effectiveness of your SEO strategy. One of the reasons why so many organizations do not use data effectively in the product design process is that all the data considered together is overwhelming. The power lies in deconstructing the mountain into smaller chunks.

Site Visitors and Bounce Rates

The motivation that a noncustomer has in becoming a customer of your business begins with them visiting your website or downloading your app, generally known as search engine optimization (SEO). The volume of traffic driven to your website is relatively easy to measure using Google Analytics or other analytics tools in the market.

The part of the motivation that is harder to track is how motivated the visiting noncustomer is to become a converted customer. We can approximate this motivation by observing how many site visitors who land on your website stay longer than the first 10 seconds: a site visitor who is not motivated will not hang around on your website. Instead, they will give it a once over, deciding swiftly if you are for them. This process takes less than 10 seconds.

At ADORE Zero and Ten Seconds, the metrics that you need to track success are:

1. SEO markers such as Google rankings
2. Number of site visitors
3. Bounce rates
4. NPS
5. Brand sentiment

Average Time on Site

If the site visitor stays on your website past the first 10 seconds, they will go on to the next milestone in the customer journey, the ADORE Three Minute milestone. For a site visitor to stay around for this amount of time, your website must have answered the question of "Why should I care?" This question is answered by the clarity of your value proposition and the unfolding of your brand story. The skills needed to achieve this cross traditional team boundaries: part storytelling, part design, part marketing, and probably part magic. Some brands get it right: Airbnb who entices us to go against everything we have ever been taught and invite a stranger into our homes; or Uber, who convinces us that our mothers were wrong and that it's totally OK to get into a car with a stranger, or Afterpay who make instant gratification and consumer debt downright desirable. These brands communicate the value proposition well and then draw us into their story—in the example of Afterpay, they focus on the "Why should I care" perfectly by displaying all of the fabulous brands that consumers want to buy (Figure 3.3). However, their home page perfectly ignores what Afterpay is and what the consequences of skipping your payments may bring.

At the ADORE Three Minutes, the metrics that you need to track to measure success are:

1. Average time on site
2. Average page visits
3. Average return visits

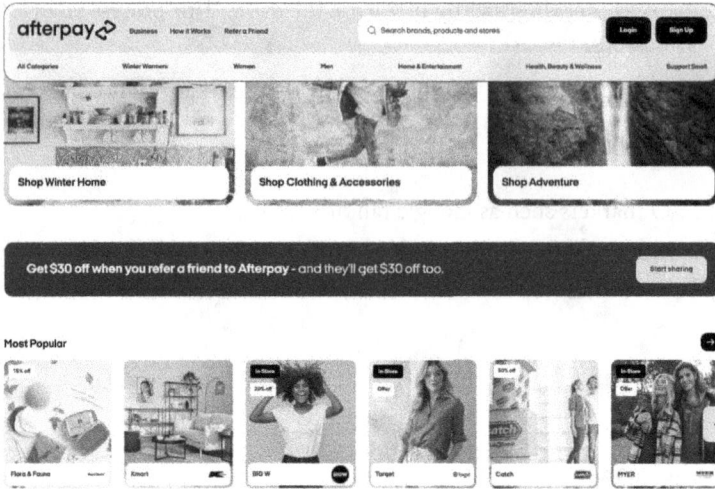

*Figure 3.3 Afterpay's home page prioritizes the "Why should I care"
by featuring desirable brands rather than focusing on the mechanics
of the service*

Depending on the nature of your product, it may take multiple
return visits to be convinced of your value—on the flip side, if site visitors
perceive no value, they won't indulge in a return visit. Losing a potential
customer at this point can hurt and result in the departed customer
spending more with your competitor.

Visitor to Sign-Up Ratio and Postsign-Up Engagement Rates

One of the fundamentals of great product design is to make it easy for
the user to succeed by reducing their homework. Homework is a combination of physical, cognitive, and emotional hurdles that are placed in
the way of getting a task done—asking the user to remember information
between screens, having a credit card entry screen that does not feel right,
placing buttons in unintuitive places, asking the user to reenter information all place a burden on your user that inhibit them from taking action.

On the other hand, there is the persuasive side of design that creates
situations that incentivize the user to click the button, which makes it easy
to take the next step—one-click buying from Amazon, easy free returns,
money-back guarantees, glowing product reviews, are all examples of

incentives that are built into successful products to nudge the noncustomer toward conversion.

At ADORE Sign-up and First 48 Hours, you can track success using these metrics:

1. Sign-up to visitor ratio
2. Postsign-up retention rates
3. Time to first success
4. Task error rates (observational)
5. Task success rates (observational)

These metrics are a little harder to collect. You will need to set up trackers inside tools like Hubspot to track 1, 2, and 3 above. Measuring task success and error rates will require you to set up an observational user test. Refer to the worksheets from Part II for tips on how to get started.

Anxiety

The mark of a great product designer is their ability to preempt the anxieties that a site visitor will experience in their journey from the first contact to becoming a loyal customer. Anxieties come up between each of the ADORE process™ milestones: for example, for a site visitor to stay past the ADORE Three Minute milestone, your design needs to have established credibility, trust, and a good sense of how your product can make their life better.

Measures of anxiety are among the most insightful metrics to collect if you are looking to improve conversion rates. It is relatively easy to measure anxiety, as it usually correlates to an exit point in the customer journey. If, for example, you have terrific metrics for site visitors, the visitors are staying on your site and signing up to your product, yet you are losing 90 percent of them in the first 48 hours (or week) after sign-on, you have identified your exit point. The exit point will correlate to a source of anxiety—you will need to dig deeper to figure out what the anxiety is specifically. In general terms, it will be a blocker that is preventing the customer from getting to a "first win."

Anxieties or the spaces between each of the ADORE milestones can be measured through these metrics:

1. Significant exit points from the customer journey

You can also use these metrics as a proxy for anxiety:

1. System Usability Scale (SUS)
2. Net Promoter Score (NPS)
3. Customer Satisfaction Score (CSAT)

The returns on identifying and fixing issues caused by anxieties often provide the greatest returns on investment. Therefore, as a rule of thumb, fix these items as a first priority in the customer journey, as the exits directly impact your cost of customer acquisition and customer lifetime value.

Applying ADORE to Digital Assets Other Than Websites

The ADORE process™ can be applied to any digital channel through which you seek to create or improve digital relationships between buyers and brands. Fundamentally, the ADORE process™ describes the emotional journey and experiences that buyers go through as they cross the chasm from stranger to brand promoter. As the process defines the system of experiences of the buyer, it is, by extension, channel-independent. The progression from stranger to buyer can take place on a website, but it can equally take place across a variety of contexts and touchpoints, including:

1. E-mail sequences and campaigns
2. In-app experiences
3. Web app experiences
4. Social media native eCommerce
5. Chatbots
6. Subdomains and landing pages

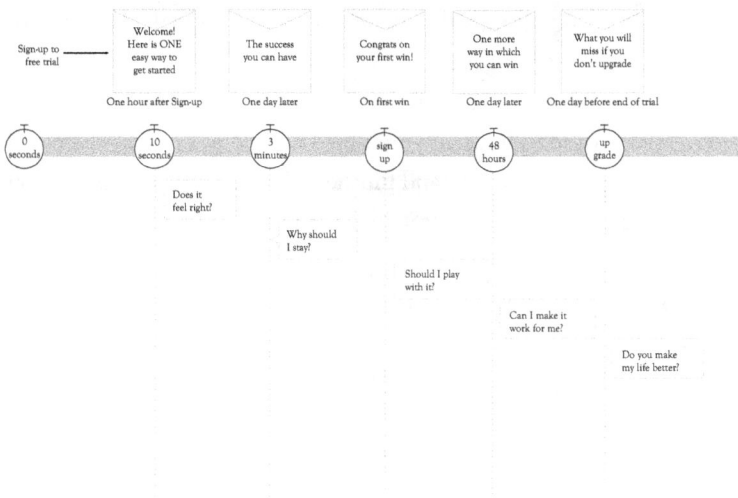

Figure 3.4 Applying the ADORE Process™ to the e-mail sequence

If you are working in a digital medium that is not the primary website, simply apply the same ADORE process™ from Part II to the medium you are working in.

Example: Working With Onboarding E-Mail Sequences

One of the most common applications of the ADORE process™ outside of the main website is in the treatment of e-mail marketing campaigns during an onboarding sequence (Figure 3.4). A typical example of this might look like this:

1. Send a *Welcome* e-mail on Sign-up to a free trial
2. Send a *Getting Started* e-mail an hour after Sign-up
3. Send a *Why People Love Us* e-mail a day later
4. Send a (slightly nervous) *We See You Are Losing Interest* e-mail two days later
5. Send a *Your Trial Has Ended, Don't Leave* e-mail seven days after sign-up

Intuitively, you will note that the e-mail sequence makes you squirm a little. The reason for this is simple: the arc of how a relationship should develop is not respected. Instead of respecting the natural cadence at which a relationship unfolds and building trust along the way, the e-mail sequence comes on too strong and finishes off with an air of desperation. Again, consider the parallels to real life, human-to-human relationships—you would run a mile. So, it is not surprising that the open rates on e-mail sequences like this one may start at 20 to 30 percent and quickly taper off to almost zero by the last e-mail.

Applying the ADORE process™, the onboarding e-mail sequence may be redesigned as:

1. Send a *Welcome. Here is one easy to get started* e-mail one hour after Sign-up for a free trial.
2. Send a *The value you can realize, and that others have realized* e-mail one day later.
3. Either
   (a) Send a *Congrats on your first win! How to achieve your next win* e-mail on completion of the first win (to guide them along to the next win).
   (b) Send a *How to achieve your first win e-mail* two days after Sign-up (if you notice that they have not completed their first win).
4. Send a *The value you have realized so far by using our product* e-mail three to four days later.
5. Either
   (a) Send an aspirational *Businesses like yours get gains like these by using our product* e-mail two days before the end of the trial period.
   (b) Send an aspirational *Let us help you to achieve these gains* e-mail two days before the end of the trial period (with instructions to a win).
6. Send a *Sign-up before your trial runs out* e-mail one day before the end of the trial period.

Note that the e-mails are spaced apart to give the newly signed up customer enough space to try to use the product. The content of the e-mails is focused on providing value and gentle guidance while building a sense of value and urgency.

The payoffs of getting your e-mail sequence optimized are as clear cut as those of getting your primary website presence optimized. Case studies from companies like Klaviyo show that effective e-mail strategies, due to their net cost of zero per e-mail sent, lead to decisive competitive advantages when they can be optimized toward "building an emotional bond with an audience of one" (Morrison 2021). Relationships are king, on the web, by e-mail and on other digital channels.

You can apply the ADORE process™ across all digital channels. Remember to identify the metrics that will indicate success at each milestone and focus on delivering value: how do you make their life better?

Using ADORE to Optimize Product Team Performance

The ADORE process™ has evolved from my work running product teams in various organizations. It has proven to be effective for delivering digital experiences that correlate to increased revenue and aligning individuals in the team to maximize the team's performance.

A good team creates magic. In *The Science of Teamwork*, the authors analyze 60 years of research into team dynamics in the military (Goodwin, Blacksmith, and Coats 2018). One of their key findings shows that a good team, a team with strong bonds between its members, can achieve more than the sum of its parts: "Teams can be more effective than the sum of individual team members. Cohesive teams (i.e., strong bonds among members) perform better and stay together longer than non-cohesive teams. Teams can absorb more task demands, perform with fewer errors, and exceed performance based on linear composites of individual performance."

"Ma" is a Japanese boundary, but it isn't a line. It is a void, an expanse. The literal translation is space between, but rather than a static gap, it is the distance that exists between objects as well as between time. It is the silent pause between the interactions between people.

—Abrahamson 2013

The bulk of my career was shaped serving in, building, and growing product teams in technology companies worldwide. Sometimes the teams worked out well and produced "magic," and sometimes they imploded. When things imploded, it was always tempting to look for what caused the failure. But, over time, I discovered that it was often *what was not there* that caused the failures. The failures were in the space between—and so were the successes.

A well-functioning product team recognizes that team performance is built on the Hum, the "ma" that exists between individuals (Harrison 2020b). The Hum is fundamentally based on trust, which is a quality of individuals and based on a foundation of trust. Because of this, each time we swap an individual in or out of a team, we affect the Hum for the team. A new Hum can be formed, but it will take time—and in that time, the productivity of the product team can be adversely affected.

One of the challenges in maintaining and rebuilding the Hum when team members change is that the turnover creates an opportunity for finger pointing and blame to creep in. Due to its objectivity and measurability, the ADORE process™ can be used effectively to transition work to individuals best suited for the job. Using the metrics at each ADORE milestone focuses energy on a shared vision of creating digital assets that increase conversion rates and build stronger relationships with buyers. Teams can be rewarded for their contributions to conversion rate uplifts, and individuals in product teams can effectively measure the value of their contributions.

Anecdotally, based on my observations and leadership of product teams, I would wager that the employee turnover on product teams would be significantly reduced if team performance was measured in this way. Sure, people move, and priorities change, but most often, a team with the Hum falls apart when people start to leave and leave behind them a wake of uncertainty. The ADORE process™ provides a framework to eliminate that.

To use the ADORE process™ to optimize the performance of your product teams:

1. Recognize that capable teams perform well when there is time to establish trust and develop the Hum.

2. When there is turnover, use the ADORE process™ as a framework to ensure work continuity.

3. Track the performance of work delivered by teams and individuals and use these as objectives measures of the contribution of your product teams.

Demonstrating Your Value as an Individual Product Team Member

According to Amazon, there will be a 79 percent increase in demand for digital workers by 2025. Along with technology, cybersecurity, and AI skills, the need for design skills to deploy digital products, services, and offerings will be in high demand. According to Dr. Fraser Thompson, director of AlphaBeta, the company that prepared the Amazon report, "The challenge is huge, but the payoff would be tremendous in terms of stronger economic growth, higher incomes, and a more equitable and resilient economy." As designers, most of us get out of bed to contribute to this vision of a shared future.

The challenge that many designers and professionals working in the digital product design sector face is that there is no standardized way to measure one's effectiveness as a designer. Design prowess is typically evaluated based on aesthetics—designers do not boast the impact their designs have on the bottom line of the business. These conditions perpetuate the systematic undervaluation of the contribution that design makes to business success. On the one hand, we know that there is a correlation between success and businesses that are design-led—on the other hand, we hire individuals into product teams based on the aesthetic of their Behance portfolio.

As a product professional, you can use the ADORE process™ to track the impact of your work. Simply remember to note the baseline metrics before your work was shipped and the metrics several months after. Then, start to track these metrics in your portfolios and encourage your colleagues to do the same. In this way, you can begin to objectively demonstrate the value that you bring to the table in your team, and collectively, the value that your team brings to the organization as a whole.

Summary

The ADORE process™ for digital brand romance described in Part II can be scaled in its application to help you run more effective product teams, and to provide a framework for engaging with external agencies and service providers. At an individual level, the ADORE process™ can be used to demonstrate your value as a designer—shifting the conversation in product design away from subjective aesthetics, to demonstrating the value of design in objective, practical, and dollar terms.

Epilogue

It is widely recognized that we live in unpredictable times, marked by an increasing rate of change. It is also widely acknowledged that as humans, we are reasonably resistant to change. These conditions create a perfect storm of fear, uncertainty, and doubt at an individual, business, and institutional level. The ADORE process™ describes a system that can build more profound, lasting, and meaningful relationships between brands and buyers. It describes a system that can be used to create digital artifacts that articulate and direct the evolution of these relationships. It provides objective metrics to track progress and de-risk your journey toward brand loyalty, repeat buys, and advocacy. The ADORE process™ provides you with the tools to conquer tomorrow's business unknowns.

Appendix

Additional Resources

All downloads available from rammp.com/digital-brand-romance

Zero Seconds

Download the Worksheets

Marketing strategy on a page
Working with Nodes
Troubleshooting guide

Watch the Video

SEO Smarts

Ten Seconds

Download the Worksheets

First Impressions: The Emotion of Color
Express value in the currency of your audience: A quick start
Write your Brand Story (the most important worksheet you will ever complete)

Watch the Video

Product Sales Mastery Lesson 1

Three Minutes

Download the Worksheets

Chart the buying process and obstacles
Home page template

Watch the Video

Product Sales Mastery Lesson 2

Sign-Up

Download the Worksheets

Identify points of perceived value
Create artifacts that make life easier

Watch the Video

Product Sales Mastery Lesson 3

First 48 Hours

Download the Worksheets

Simple usability testing tips
Time to first success
Value matrix

Watch the Video

Product Sales Mastery Lesson 4
Usability Test Like a #Boss

Upgrade

Download the Worksheets

Create value add shareable artifacts

Watch the Video

Product Sales Mastery Lesson 5

Recommend, or RIP

Download the Worksheets

Understand why they leave

Watch the Video

Product Sales Mastery Lesson 6

Share Your Story

Share your experience with the ADORE process™—we all learn from each other, and everyone enjoys a great story!

References

Ansari, A., and E. Klinenberg. 2016. *Modern Romance*. Penguin Books. www.amazon.com.au/Modern-Romance-Aziz-Ansari/dp/0143109251

Arcieri, K. 2021. "Amazon Could See Revenue More than Double by 2025 as Retail Business Grows." S&P Global Market Intelligence. www.spglobal.com/marketintelligence/en/news-insights/latest-news-headlines/amazon-could-see-revenue-more-than-double-by-2025-as-retail-business-grows-62718086

Ariely, D. 2010. *Predictably Irrational: The Hidden Forces That Shape Our Decisions*. Harper Perennial. www.amazon.com/Predictably-Irrational-Revised-Expanded-Decisions/dp/0061353248

Aron, A., E. Melinat, E. Aron, R.D. Vallone, and R. Bator. 1997. "The Experimental Generation of Interpersonal Closeness: A Procedure and Some Preliminary Findings." SAGE Social Science Collections. https://journals.sagepub.com/doi/pdf/10.1177/0146167297234003?hc_location=ufi

Ashraf, N., C.F. Camerer, and G. Loewenstein. 2005. "Adam Smith, Behavioral Economist." *Journal of Economic Perspectives* 19, no. 3, pp. 131–45. https://doi.org/10.1257/089533005774357897

Berger, J. 2020. *The Catalyst*. Simon & Schuster. www.amazon.com.au/Catalyst-How-Change-Anyones-Mind-ebook/dp/B07THCZ626

Bohlen, J.M., and G. M. Beal. 1957. "The Diffusion Process." *Special Report No. 18*, no. 1, pp. 56–77. https://lib.dr.iastate.edu/cgi/viewcontent.cgi?article=1015&context=specialreports

Catron, M.L. 2015. "To Fall in Love with Anyone, Do This." *The New York Times*, www.nytimes.com/2015/01/11/style/modern-love-to-fall-in-love-with-anyone-do-this.html

Cialdini, R. 2006. *Influence: The Psychology of Persuasion, Revised Edition*. Archives of Internal Medicine.

Collins, J. 2001. *Good to Great: Why Some Companies Make the Leap and Others Don't*. HarperBusiness. www.amazon.com.au/Good-Great-Some-Companies-Others/dp/0066620996

De Botton, A. 2017. *The Course of Love*. Penguin (General UK). www.amazon.com.au/Course-Love-Alain-Botton/dp/0241962137

Der Hovanesian, M. 1999. "Coming on Strong." *Wall Street Journal*, www.wsj.com/articles/SB942785816835228037

Edelman, D. 2010. "Branding in the Digital Age: You're Spending Your Money in All the Wrong Places." *Harvard Business Review*, https://hbr.org/2010/12/branding-in-the-digital-age-youre-spending-your-money-in-all-the-wrong-places

Goodwin, G.F., N. Blacksmith, and M.R. Coats. 2018. "The Science of Teams in the Military: Contributions from Over 60 Years of Research." *American Psychologist*, https://doi.org/10.1037/amp0000259

Harrison, A. 2015. "Principles of Experience Design for Airport Terminals." Queensland University of Technology. https://eprints.qut.edu.au/83947/

Harrison, A. 2020a. "7 Common UX Testing Mistakes, and How to Avoid Them." UX Collective. https://uxdesign.cc/7-common-ux-testing-mistakes-and-how-to-avoid-them-8ed73ee9ab5e

Harrison, A. 2020b. "How to Scale High Performance Product Teams." UX Collective. https://uxdesign.cc/how-to-scale-high-performance-product-teams-78e702d2f3fb

Harrison, A. 2021. "The Critical SEO Factors That Google and Facebook Don't Want You to Know about." Better Marketing. https://bettermarketing.pub/the-critical-seo-factors-that-google-and-facebook-dont-want-you-to-know-about-596d1a3bd3f4

Harvard Business Review. July–August 2020. July 1, 2020. https://store.hbr.org/product/harvard-business-review-july-august-2020/BR2004

Harvard Business Review. March–April 2021. https://hbr.org/archive-toc/BR2102

Heim, A. 2021. "How Bottom-up Sales Helped Expensify Blaze the Path for SaaS | TechCrunch." ExtraCrunch. https://techcrunch.com/2021/06/08/expensify-ec1-business/

"How Grammarly Quietly Grew Its Way to 6.9 Million Daily Users in 9 Years." 2017. Product Habits Blog. https://producthabits.com/how-grammarly-quietly-grew-its-way-to-7-million-daily-users/

Jacoby, J., and D.B. Kyner. 1973. "Brand Loyalty vs. Repeat Purchasing Behavior." *Journal of Marketing Research* 10, no. 1, p. 9. https://doi.org/10.2307/3149402

John, L.K. 2021. "Savvy Self-Promotion." Harvard Business Review. https://hbr.org/2021/05/savvy-self-promotion

Johnson, J. 2021. "Google: Ad Revenue 2001–2018." Statista. www.statista.com/statistics/266249/advertising-revenue-of-google/

Kahneman, D. 2013. *Thinking, Fast and Slow*. Farrar, Strauss, and Giroux. www.amazon.com/Thinking-Fast-Slow-Daniel-Kahneman/dp/0374533555

Kim, L. 2021. "What Is a Good Conversion Rate? It's Higher Than You Think!" Wordstream. www.wordstream.com/blog/ws/2014/03/17/what-is-a-good-conversion-rate

Krockow, E. September 27, 2018. "How Many Decisions Do We Make Each Day?" *Psychology Today.* www.psychologytoday.com/au/blog/stretching-theory/201809/how-many-decisions-do-we-make-each-day

Labad, J., A. González-Rodríguez, J. Cobo, J. Puntí, and J.M. Farré. January 2021. "A Systematic Review and Realist Synthesis on Toilet Paper Hoarding: COVID or Not COVID, That Is the Question." *PeerJ.* https://doi.org/10.7717/PEERJ.10771

Lecinski, J. 2011. "Winning the Zero Moment of Truth." Think With Google. www.thinkwithgoogle.com/future-of-marketing/emerging-technology/2011-winning-zmot-ebook/

Ludden, D. 2017. "The Psychology of First Impressions." *Psychology Today Australia,* www.psychologytoday.com/au/blog/talking-apes/201708/the-psychology-first-impressions

Manu, A. 2007. *The Imagination Challenge: Strategic Foresight and Innovation in the Global Economy.* Peachpit Press. www.amazon.ca/Imagination-Challenge-Strategic-Foresight-Innovation/dp/0321413652/ref=sr_1_3?crid=2GBU3IAUDQLU9&keywords=alexander+manu&qid=1636415754&s=books&sprefix=Alexander+Manu%2Cstripbooks%2C79&sr=1-3

Manu, A. 2017. *Transforming Organizations for the Subscription Economy : Starting from Scratch.* Routledge. www.amazon.com.au/Transforming-Organizations-Subscription-Economy-Starting/dp/1138281700

Markey, R. 2020. "Are You Undervaluing Your Customers?" *Harvard Business Review.* https://hbr.org/2020/01/are-you-undervaluing-your-customers

Markman, A. 2015. "Influence People by Leveraging the Brain's Laziness." *Harvard Business Review.* May 29. https://hbr.org/2015/05/influence-people-by-leveraging-the-brains-laziness

Maslow, A. H. 1966. *Psychology of Science.* HarperCollins. www.amazon.com/Psychology-Science-Abraham-Harold-Maslow/dp/0060341459

Moore, G. E. April 1965. "Cramming More Components onto Integrated Circuits." *Electronics,* https://newsroom.intel.com/wp-content/uploads/sites/11/2018/05/moores-law-electronics.pdf

Mori, N. 2008. "Styles of Remembering and Types of Experience: An Experimental Investigation of Reconstructive Memory." *Integrative Psychological & Behavioral Science* 42, no. 3, pp. 291–314. https://doi.org/10.1007/S12124-008-9068-5

Morrison, C. 2021. "Marketing in 2021 Is Emotional and Not Just Transactional." Extra Crunch. https://techcrunch.com/2021/04/19/klaviyo-ec1-marketing/

Nicholson, N. August 1998. "How Hardwired Is Human Behavior?" Harvard Business Review. https://hbr.org/1998/07/how-hardwired-is-human-behavior

Norman, D.A. 2009. "Designing Waits That Work." *MIT Sloan Management Review*. https://sloanreview.mit.edu/article/designing-waits-that-work/

Ordun, G. 2015. "Millennial (Gen Y) Consumer Behavior, Their Shopping Preferences and Perceptual Maps Associated with Brand Loyalty." *Canadian Social Science* 11, no. 4, pp. 40–55. https://doi.org/10.3968/6697

Parment, A. 2013. "Generation Y vs. Baby Boomers: Shopping Behavior, Buyer Involvement and Implications for Retailing." *Journal of Retailing and Consumer Services* 20, no. 2, pp. 189–199. https://doi.org/10.1016/J.JRETCONSER.2012.12.001

Pine, J., and J. Gilmore. 1998. "Welcome to the Experience Economy." *Harvard Business Review*. https://hbr.org/1998/07/welcome-to-the-experience-economy

Quelch, J., and K.E. Jocz. April 2009. "How to Market in a Downturn." *Harvard Business Review*. https://hbr.org/2009/04/how-to-market-in-a-downturn-2

Ross, A., and M. Tyler. 2011. *Predictable Revenue: Turn Your Business into a Sales Machine with the $100 Million Best Practices of Salesforce.Com*. PebbleStorm. www.amazon.com.au/Predictable-Revenue-Business-Practices-Salesforce-com/dp/0984380213

Samson, A. 2017. "The Behavioral Economics Guide." http://eprints.lse.ac.uk/84059/1/The%20behavioral%20economics%20guide%202017.pdf

Schewan, D. 2021. "How Much Does Google Ads Cost?" Wordstream. www.wordstream.com/blog/ws/2015/05/21/how-much-does-adwords-cost

Schwartz, E. 1997. *Webonomics*. Broadway Books. www.evanischwartz.com/webonomics

Sinek, S. 2009. *Start with Why: How Great Leaders Inspire Everyone to Take Action*. Penguin. https://simonsinek.com/product/start-with-why/

Taniguchi, N. 2021. "How COVID Changed Consumer's Decision Journey." Think With Google. www.thinkwithgoogle.com/consumer-insights/consumer-journey/covid-decision-journey/

Voss, C. 2016. *Never Split the Difference: Negotiating as If Your Life Depended on It*. Harper Business. www.amazon.com/Never-Split-Difference-Negotiating-Depended/dp/0062407805

Acknowledgments

In *Big Magic*, Elizabeth Gilbert beautifully personifies ideas. She describes them as dormant beings that exist in the spaces between us, searching for nothing more than a human host to bring them to life. An idea may tap you on the shoulder, and you may ignore it, only to see it brought to life by a competitor in another country. The idea you ignored simply kept looking for a willing human host.

Elements of what you have read in this book had their inception points while I ran product teams at Tiny and Scrunch and worked on projects with WordPress and IBM. These early idea seedlings were further grown during my PhD sabbatical, which allowed me the intellectual luxury of learning more deeply about behavioral economics, psychology, design, and experience. I am extremely grateful to my colleagues and friends from this time for the hundreds of conversations and experiments that helped me to shape tomorrow's ideas. More recently, I have had the privilege of working with over 80 of New Zealand Trade and Enterprise's best export customers. This singular opportunity, overlaid with the challenges of remote work imposed on us all by COVID-19, helped to accelerate and refine 20 years of thinking into what is now the patent-pending ADORE process™. Thank you, Alan, Glen, Gabrielle, Greg, Pam, Katie, Hamish, Stuart, Christine, Vanessa, and Ben, for your support and for the unique privilege of working with your progressive customers and team.

Sincere thanks to Prof. Naresh Malhotra, Senior Fellow, Georgia Tech Center for International Business Education and Research and Regents' Professor Emeritus, Georgia Institute of Technology (Georgia Tech) for his feedback and direction during the course of preparing this manuscript, and to Scott Isenberg, Business Expert Press, for your guidance and support. No doubt this is only the first of our work together. A big thank you to Karina Harrison and Greg Harrison for their insightful comments and review of the early manuscript, and to Prof. Alexander Manu for perfectly pointed feedback at critical junctures as the book was evolving.

On a personal note, a huge thanks to my parents, Basia and Michal Andrusiewicz, who showed me that there is value in learning, exploring, traveling, dreaming, and doing, even in the face of unknowns; and a heart full of gratitude to my partner in work and in life, Steve White, for listening with patience, cooking with love, and making all of the ideas brighter with his boundless optimism and creative energy.

About the Author

Dr. Anna Harrison is a top-ranked digital technology advisor, product expert, and author. Anna's work has helped New Zealand's best exporting and emerging brands create strategic and measurable plans to accelerate growth in new markets. Supported by successes across Europe, Asia, and the United States, Anna's work will help you remove your reliance on luck in the future success of your brand.

Index

OTHER TITLES IN THE MARKETING COLLECTION

Naresh Malhotra, Georgia Tech, Editor

- *Brand Vision* by Jim Everhart
- *Brand Naming* by Meyerson Rob
- *Fast Fulfillment* by Sanchoy Das
- *Multiply Your Business Value Through Brand & AI* by Rajan Narayan
- *Branding & AI* by Chahat Aggarwal
- *The Business Design Cube* by Rajagopal
- *Customer Relationship Management* by Michael Pearce
- *Stand Out!* by Brian McGurk
- *The Coming Age of Robots* by George Pettinico and George R. Milne
- *Market Entropy* by Rajagopal Rajagopal
- *Decoding Customer Value at the Bottom of the Pyramid* by Ritu Srivastava
- *Qualitative Marketing Research* by Rajagopal

Concise and Applied Business Books

The Collection listed above is one of 30 business subject collections that Business Expert Press has grown to make BEP a premiere publisher of print and digital books. Our concise and applied books are for...

- Professionals and Practitioners
- Faculty who adopt our books for courses
- Librarians who know that BEP's Digital Libraries are a unique way to offer students ebooks to download, not restricted with any digital rights management
- Executive Training Course Leaders
- Business Seminar Organizers

Business Expert Press books are for anyone who needs to dig deeper on business ideas, goals, and solutions to everyday problems. Whether one print book, one ebook, or buying a digital library of 110 ebooks, we remain the affordable and smart way to be business smart. For more information, please visit www.businessexpertpress.com, or contact sales@businessexpertpress.com.

www.ingramcontent.com/pod-product-compliance
Lightning Source LLC
Chambersburg PA
CBHW061739270326
41928CB00011B/2302